THE POWER
— OF —
SELF-BELIEF

CAREN PASKEL

The Power of Self-Belief © Copyright 2022 Caren Paskel

www.rosenpotter.com

All rights reserved. No part of this publication may be reproduced, distributed, or transmitted in any form or by any means, including photocopying, recording, or other electronic or mechanical methods, without the prior written permission of the publisher, except in the case of brief quotations embodied in critical reviews and certain other noncommercial uses permitted by copyright law.

Although the author and publisher have made every effort to ensure that the information in this book was correct at press time, the author and publisher do not assume and hereby disclaim any liability to any party for any loss, damage, or disruption caused by errors or omissions, whether such errors or omissions result from negligence, accident, or any other cause.

Adherence to all applicable laws and regulations, including international, federal, state, and local governing professional licensing, business practices, advertising, and all other aspects of doing business in the US, Canada, or any other jurisdiction is the sole responsibility of the reader and consumer.

Neither the author nor the publisher assumes any responsibility or liability whatsoever on behalf of the consumer or reader of this material. Any per-ceived slight of any individual or organization is purely unintentional.

The resources in this book are provided for informational purposes only and should not be used to replace the specialized training and professional judgment of a health care or mental health care professional.

Neither the author nor the publisher can be held responsible for the use of the information provided within this book. Please always consult a trained professional before making any decision regarding the treatment of yourself or others.

For more information, email cmp@carenpaskel.com

ISBN: 979-8-9863600-0-3

Get The Video Summary & Bonus Course Bundle Free!

READ THIS FIRST

To say thank you for reading my book, I would like to give you access to the audio version, video summary, additional training, and my mini-course for you to continue evolving on your journey of self-belief 100% FREE!

I know you are more likely to finish the book if you have supporting material and if I was narrating and coaching with you so it feels like we are having an intimate conversation.

Instead of paying $997+ for this bundle, I want you to have it for free…

>>> *www.carenpaskel.com/book-bundle* <<<

The Power of Self-Belief

Self-belief enables you to transform yourself, your life, and the world.

By Caren Paskel

Why and Who This is for...

When my husband died of brain cancer at thirty years of age, I had a choice to focus on what was lost and all of the pain or what was received and all of the blessings. I could live a lost and painful existence or a receptive and blessed one. From the power of self-belief, I chose the latter. Deciding to believe in myself awakened my inner power to show up fully, shine and share the story. My late husband's sole purpose was to make a positive impact on others. His self-belief inspired finding mine. *The Power of Self-Belief* is written in the spirit of reciprocation. I am being called upon to honor and keep his mission alive.

The Power of Self-Belief is for one and all, no matter who you are or where you're from. The book is an approachable way to inspire your self-belief and spread the message to the masses without wasting precious time and energy. Self-belief cannot be bought, sold, or given. Traditional education, degrees, credentials, and certificates are unnecessary. Power exists inside every human being. You must uncover to discover. All you need to do is look within. Yes, it's that simple that you may pass it off. But it's the truth. With self-belief anything's possible. Without self-belief everything's impossible. Self-limiting beliefs limit your immense potential. Staying small stunts both material and spiritual growth. Growth happens as a result of self-belief and self-love (that's my next book!)

Believing in yourself provides the ability to make essential shifts and changes for an extraordinary and exceptional life. Self-belief is the main ingredient for happiness, peace, and prosperity. Every human can have and deserves all three. The power of self-belief enables radical transformation on every level; physically, mentally, intellectually, and spiritually. My intention of writing is to empower your self-belief and educate on Universal laws through storytelling. *The Power of Self-Belief* is my true story interwoven with timeless teachings and values that have taken over two decades of consistent study and education under masters on the subject to embody and exemplify. The world shall no longer be deprived. May *The Power of Self-Belief* uplift and create more harmony and union over disharmony and separation. A ripple effect will evoke worldly transformation one by one.

Contents

Acknowledgments x

Introduction 1

Phase One | Brain Cancer Plus Big Love..............................**3**

The Deadly Diagnosis 3

    Power-Thought: Infinite Love..4

The Entrepreneurial Endeavors 5

    Power-Thought: Follow Your Conviction 6

The Real Estate Plan 7

    Power-Thought: Sacrifice Strengthens Relationships...................8

The Dogs 9

    Power-Thought: With Growth Comes Outgrowth 10

The Great Dane..11

    Power-Thought: Happiness Resides Inside 15

The Massive Seizure 16

    Power-Thought: Find and Seek Hidden Blessings 19

The Housemate 19

    Power-Thought: Trust Divine Timing 21

The First Brain Tumor 21

    Power-Thought: Determination Drives You Forward 25

Phase Two | Overseas Overwhelm Plus Moving Madness..............**27**

The Ireland Issues..27

    Power-Thought: Complaining Is Draining 28

The Missed MRI..29

    Power-Thought: You Become What You Focus On 30

The South Africa Shift 31

    Power Thought: Self-Belief Conquers Self-Limiting Beliefs 35

The Moving Disaster 35

    Power-Thought: A Warrior Beats a Worrier 37

Phase Three | Holiday Hell Plus Deadly Diagnosis.............................**39**

The Homecoming Mayhem 39

    Power-Thought: Breakdowns Lead to Breakthroughs 40

The Christmas Crisis 41

    Power-Thought: Save Your Own Ass First 42

The Reunion 43
    Power-Thought: Allow for Breathing Room 44
The Terminal Tumor 45
    Power-Thought: Decide to Thrive 46
The Pancreatitis Scare 47
    Power-Thought: Self-Preserve to Serve Others 49

Phase Four | Pandemic Pivots Plus Top Brain Cancer Team 51
The Shut Down... 51
    Power-Thought: Closing Doors Opens New Ones 53
The True Calling 53
    Power-Thought: Change Is a Wake-Up Call.................... 56
The Appointment 56
    Power-Thought: Perseverance Provides Inner Vigor 59
The Pandemic Peeves 59
    Power-Thought: Become Evolved and Not Involved 60
The Good Results 61
    Power-Thought: Goals for Your Expansion 63

Phase Five | Roles Reversed Plus Endings.............................65
The Revival 65
    Power-Thought: Be A Winner Not a Whiner 67
The Spark 67
    Power-Thought: Self-Limiting Beliefs Breed Limitations.............. 69
The Studio Closing.. 70
    Power-Thought: Staying Small Stunts Your Growth.................... 71
The Last Birthday 72
    Power-Thought: The Greatest Gift Is Life.......................... 74

Phase Six | Family Dynamics Plus House of Gathering 77
The Families 77
    Power-Thought: Adapting and Adjusting Is a Skill 79
The Family Emails... 80
    Power-Thought: Use Effective Communication 83
The Friends.. 84
    Power-Thought: Wisely Choose Your Friends 86
The Friend Circle.. 87
    Power-Thought: Build Your Army of Support...................... 90

The Food 90

    Power-Thought: Quality of Life Over Quantity..............................92

Phase Seven | Divine Orchestration Plus Final Countdown 93

The Divine Goodbye 93

    Power-Thought: Reach for Your Greatest Potential 94

The Last MRI..95

    Power-Thought: Show Up Rather Than Give Up 97

The Move Downstairs...97

    Power-Thought: Trust Your Judgment....................................99

The Caregiver and Hospice Angels....................................100

    Power-Thought: Attracting Earth Angels 101

The Last Ten Days 102

    Power-Thought: Honor Your Journey....................................104

The Last Supper..104

    Power-Thought: Live to Be Giving 105

The Last Prayer...106

    Power-Thought: Self-Belief Is Reunion..................................107

The Epic Seizure 108

    Power-Thought: Nature Has a Plan.....................................110

The Last Breath...110

    Power-Thought: Death Is Rebirth..112

Phase Eight | Celebrations Plus Life After Loss................................113

The Million Dollar Death 113

    Power-Thought: Self-Belief Brings Abundance 114

The Celebration of Life 115

    Power-Thought: A Wave in The Sea of Life 120

The After Death Holidays 120

    Power-Thought: Celebrate Life Every Day 121

Phase Nine | New Openings Plus New Beginnings..........................123

The Loft...123

    Power-Thought: Believe and Receive..................................124

The Waiting Room...124

    Power-Thought: Make A Shift That Lifts................................125

The Solo Getaways 126

    Power-Thought: The World Is a Playground 128

viii

The Home Alone 129

 Power-Thought: Lead the Way 130

Phase Ten | Full Unveiling Plus Double Metamorphosis **133**

The Vail Trip Together 133

 Power-Thought: Dream While You're Awake...........................136
The Vail Trip Alone...136

 Power-Thought: Share Your Story..................................138
The Brain Cancer Connections..138

 Power-Thought: Spread Cheer Over Fear 140
The Ski Tours...141

 Power-Thought: You Attract What You Are..............................142
The Butterfly Queen..143

 Power Thought: Your Light Brightens the World 144

Phase Eleven | The Power of Self-Love to Be Continued… **145**

The Love After Loss 145

 Power-Thought: You Hold the Key to Unlock Your Heaven....146

About the Author: **147**

Resources **148**

Acknowledgments

- **My Beloved Late Husband David Prentice**
  - Thank you. Without knowing you, I would still be hiding out in my bubble. Your self-belief was magnetizing and your greatest attribute. Thankfully, that drew me to marry you. As our relationship grew and evolved, the power of your self-belief empowered my self-belief. Thanks to yours, mine was recognized. I live, work and write with gratitude and in devotional service to you. Most of all, thank you for *The Power of Self-Belief* as our legacy for the world to have and hold.

- **My Parents Marlene and Clifford Paskel**
  - Thank you. Without you, I would not be here! Thank you for raising me and taking such wonderful care of me. Thank you for your extensive love. Thank you for providing everything needed and more to grow into my best self. Your support has made it possible for me to move toward the power of my self-belief. Most of all, thank you for giving me the grandest gift of all, life.

- **My Sister Lianne Paskel**
  - Thank you. You are always looking out for and protecting me. Thank you for taking extra care of me when mom and dad had their hands and plates full;) Thank you for loving me and being there for me whenever I need my big sis. Most of all, thank you for your ambition in pursuing your career and goals, in addition to raising four beautiful children with your wonderful husband.

☀ **My Brother Eric Paskel**

⊙ Thank you. You are my soul-bro. Thank you for leading the way, opening a business, and hiring me. Thank you for being my brother, teacher, and best friend. Thank you for always accepting me for me. Thank you for providing opportunities to learn and grow in myself and my career. Most of all, thank you for going on your journey to India, bringing home *Vedanta*, and sharing a Guru. This catapulted my entire life to take my journey.

☀ **My Gurus Swami A. Parthasarathy and Sunanda Leelaram**

⊙ Thank you. Spiritual Education and essential Eternal values have allowed me to live my life happily and prosperously. Thank you for laying out a practical roadmap for material and spiritual growth and evolution. The straightforward solution saved me from making poor choices, suffering the consequences, and being miserable. Most of all, thank you for making the knowledge accessible for me to live my best life and teach others to do the same.

☀ **My Mentors Ivan Rose and Solomon Potter**

⊙ Thank you. You spotted my need for your expertise and guidance on my path to personal and business development. Thank you for knowing how to encourage, support, and lovingly push me forward in such a playful way. Thank you for seeing the very best in me. Most of all, thank you for being the living unconditional presence of self-belief in David's physical absence.

INTRODUCTION

Where it all Began…

There are only two humans that I've come across who fully believed in themselves, my guru Swamiji and my late husband. The knowledge to live by, handed down from my guru, integrated throughout this book for your reflection, is what got me unstuck. I was able to set the right direction for my life and take the right actions for my evolution; exiting an unhealthy relationship that ended in divorce, quitting my job of eleven years that was the foundation of my career, getting off all medications, rising above food addiction, overcoming various health issues, opening my own business with zero experience or education, finding true love, and enjoying a wonderful marriage. I became happier, healthier, and more peaceful with less stress, worry, anxiety, and fear. My intellectual strength and stamina guided me to live a great life.

Loving, marrying, and living with someone having the power of self-belief catapulted me to even greater heights. David's undeniable self-belief was captivating. He was bursting with self-confidence. He was a magnetizing force of nature. The beginning of our relationship planted seeds that sprouted and grew into *The Power of Self-Belief* after David passed. The book holds both our narrative and essential values to live by that metamorphosed my entire existence; physical health, emotional poise, intellectual strength, financial abundance, flourishing and dynamic relationships, and an impactful career in perfect alignment with my soul's purpose.

PTs are *Power Thoughts,* and PQs are *Power Quotes*. They are at the bottom of each section to recap and break down the crucial concepts or higher value embedded. Your independent thinking is strongly encouraged to update past self-limiting beliefs or knowledge that may

Caren Paskel

no longer serve your highest self and life goals. Assimilating and living knowledge gained is wisdom. Those who know so much without being able to utilize and apply their knowledge are merely intelligent computers. Rather than simply reading and remembering the PTs and PQs, work to TRAA; Think, Reflect, Absorb and Apply. Take the time to allow for assimilation. Enjoy the freedom of thinking for yourself rather than following the herd mentality. Have fun bringing out your inner uniqueness and badass!

PHASE ONE

Brain Cancer Plus Big Love

The Deadly Diagnosis

When my husband came up the stairs with his younger brother Daniel to reveal the shocking and devastating news of the pathology report, I lost my breath. David's second surgically removed brain tumor returned as a grade four glioblastoma, the deadliest form of brain cancer. At that moment everything froze. This was not supposed to happen. Brain cancer was not in our plans. We just started our lives together, got married, and had barely scratched the surface of our lives individually and as a unit.

When we met, David believed in me more than I believed in myself. My husband's self-belief was ENORMOUS. He lacked the traditional education that most successful people had and grew up without all the material things that I had. The power of his self-belief scared the living crap out of me. His BIG thinking, desires, and dreams to make a HUGE impact terrified me. When we met at first glance, I recognized

the power of self-belief in David's bold smile. Love, at first sight, is more of an expression, that happened to us. We never looked back and only drove each other forward to build an incredible relationship, marriage, and life together.

Our love for one another was, is, and always will be pure and boundless. True love can only be given and received from self-love, (my next book). Self-love is unchanging. We were empowered by our love for one another rather than dependent. In other words, we complemented one another. What seemed to be the worst news and worst-case scenario, brought us closer together and took a remarkable turn in our lives.

Power-Thought: Infinite Love

- Pure love lasts forever. Love that's impure fades. If your love isn't infinite, it's not love.

- Pure love is unselfish and unlimited. Impure love has a shelf-life and is limited.
- Pure and selfless love creates peace and harmony internally and externally. Impure and selfish love creates disturbance and disharmony internally and externally.
- Pure love arrives from self-love.
- Self-love recognizes the greatest congruent force and source within you and all beings. When you tap into yours, you tap into Universal love.
- The concept of self-love will be expounded upon in the upcoming sequel, *The Power of Self-Love*.

Power-Quote: "When your love toward another is pure, you grow together rather than apart."

~**Caren Paskel**

The Entrepreneurial Endeavors

David and I grew together in our relationship and our careers. We met during a transitional period. I was working for my brother's company as the head yoga instructor and manager of teacher development. My role developed over eleven years along with a following of yoga students and clients. I was making a decent living with benefits, which is very rare in the fitness and wellness industry. As the business expanded to multiple locations, there was disagreement and controversy amongst company ownership. My brother and his mission were discouraged, and he was being forced out. I was caught in the middle of an internal yoga war. My livelihood and community were being threatened. It felt like a massive divorce. The company was going in a different direction and swaying me to become the leader and take over my brother's role. My conviction remains steady, as well as my fierce loyalty to my brother. The company's new mission no longer lined up with mine. With integrity, I exited the company.

Initially, without the full power of self-belief, I clung to my brother and what he had built to move forward. We decided to open our yoga studios, his in California and mine in Michigan. We would share a name and brand with a common mission and continue teaching in each other's studios and co-facilitating teacher training. Fear of failure and staying small kept me in the shadows. David saw right through the B.S. that was blocking me from being my brand. He knew it was a lack of self-belief. But I was too scared to do that! I couldn't fathom my success in opening or owning a yoga studio without being tied to my brother.

Everything David wanted to do, he did. Pushback from others never swayed him. He believed the impossible was possible despite what others said. Instead of thinking why me, he thought, why not me? Instead of thinking he could not do something he thought, *Can't Doesn't*

Exist, which his dad instilled in him and became the title of his book before he died. I borrowed the belief he had in me to open my yoga studio. With no prior business education, I counted on David and my brother to help me figure it out. Depending on their belief in me, I opened up *EnSoul Yoga* studio! David told me, "You have nothing to lose" and he was right. With him by my side, I felt more supported and less scared and alone. Plus, David was opening and running a business of his own. We went through our entrepreneurial endeavors together as a team even though our businesses were separate.

Power-Thought: Follow Your Conviction

- In life, you must set the right direction or path to know which roads to take and turns to make. Without direction, you either end up stuck or all over the place. Neither one gets you anywhere.
- Conviction is a combination of knowledge, purpose, and passion.
- To develop a conviction, use intellectual reasoning for your clarity.
  - Let intellect, and not merely likes, dislikes, feelings, and impulses of the mind, decide on your course of action. You and you alone must come to your conclusion.
- Once you have a strong conviction, your choices must align.
- You may follow others who are leading the way to honor your conviction.
  - For your inspiration, choose to be around those living the life you want to live.
- Often, those who have a powerful conviction in life, become leaders themselves.
- Being true to yourself means following your conviction in life. As Shakespeare puts it, "To thine own self be true…"

> *Power-Quote: "A 'No' uttered from the deepest conviction is better than a 'Yes' merely uttered to please, or worse, to avoid trouble."*
>
> ~Mahatma Gandhi

The Real Estate Plan

David's belief in himself and strong conviction propelled his real estate business. He planned everything for success. Purchasing and owning any home we were going to reside in was a business opportunity. He desired to have multiple homes in multiple states and countries. Over the course of his life, David lived in a variety of homes from a trailer home to a mansion. He was constantly moving and extremely adaptable. For me, the home was a nesting place. The thought of moving around was unsettling. I was not as adaptable. But I believed in David and his plan for us; to buy a home to reside in for two years for tax purposes, make renovations and improvements, and finally sell for profit. I was willing to sacrifice my individual wants for our future. Being a team player, I went along for the moving ride.

Before tying the knot, we thought it was important to live under the same roof. We were both alphas in our homes and needed to figure out how to live together before saying "I do". We agreed on an easy commute to work from our home. He asked if I would want to live in a gorgeous area of Detroit called the University District where the homes were all over a hundred years old and looked like mini castles. David wanted to provide a beautiful home for me no matter how much time we lived in it. The area was exactly as he explained. We found our first mini castle to live in for the next two years. It was on Parkside Street located directly behind the DGC; *Detroit Golf Club* that we were members of for a short period.

7

Unlike me, David did not grow up belonging to a country club and was new to this experience. He wasn't a golfer either, which had no bearing on his decision to become one. After a couple of lessons and a lot of daily practice, David was an adequate golfer! We went on golf and dinner dates and had a blast. He took his friends, family, and business partners to the club. He was very proud to be a member! Believing in himself gave David the power to do anything he put his mind to. When others thought, "no way", he proved them wrong every time with a big fat grin.

Power-Thought: Sacrifice Strengthens Relationships

- ☼ To be successful in your relationships, you have to do many things you may not want to do or even like to do. You have to make sacrifices. Those sacrifices will strengthen both you and your relationships.
    - ⊙ The outcome will be beneficial for both parties!
- ☼ Making sacrifices in a relationship builds your relationships up rather than tearing them down. Catering to appease or please is unsustainable and will end up hurting you and the relationship.
- ☼ Sacrifice is a service. Keep this attitude and your relationships will rise and strengthen to greater heights.

☀ Always have your goals in mind to make the necessary sacrifices, in your relationships, to achieve them.

> *Power-Quote: "Great achievement is usually born of great sacrifice and is never the result of selfishness."*

~**Napoleon Hill**

The Dogs

Living with my two dogs was a major sacrifice for both David and me. This was one of the biggest accommodations we had to make while living together. David wasn't a dog person, whereas I treated my dogs as if they were my children. David found my behavior toward my two boxers, Bugsy and Kylie, to be highly annoying. He was uninterested and slightly agitated by them. Until I met David, I honestly believed that anyone who was not madly in love with my dogs was not a match for me! David changed that self-limiting belief.

Moving in together with two spoiled pups caused much tension. We both had to make adjustments. For instance, my dogs and I were used to all sleeping together, under the covers... In our new home together, we agreed per David, that the dogs were not allowed upstairs. David wanted them to live in the basement or outside, NO WAY! We met in the middle. The dogs would remain on the main floor. He agreed to occasionally let the dogs out or feed them when I wasn't home. He did that for me. We both had to adapt to live all together and make it work. This was a true test of our devotion to one another.

My husband's sanity was a higher priority than my fur babies. Desiring to grow myself and my relationship with my husband replaced my obsession with owning pets. I dropped the need to have dogs in the future. For my entire life, my mind had me convinced that I could not be happy living without dogs! Another self-limiting belief. My husband's well-being and the health of our marriage were more important. Liberated from the yearning and wanting for dogs, I had no resentment toward David. This was a MEGA mark of growth for me, and I had no idea what was about to arrive!

Power-Thought: With Growth Comes Outgrowth

- ☼ You don't have to give anything up! When you grow, you outgrow. As long as you keep growing, outgrowing will naturally occur. You will outgrow what no longer serves your best self and life.

- ☼ Everyone has it backward. To truly STOP doing something, rather than giving it up, you must START doing something else. This is a replacement.

- ☼ With growth, you don't have to run after anything, as everything comes to you!

- ☼ By taking up something higher, what's below will automatically drop. Outgrowth is an effect of Growth. Voila!

- ☼ Renunciation is growth. When you grow into higher echelons of life, the lower detachments; people, places, and things no longer have power over you and fall off.

- ⊙ You won't be pulled away and lured by harmful cravings, habits, and addictions. They will go away on their own...

- ☀ Be cautious. If you think you have grown but still WANT, you have not outgrown what you are wanting. When you no longer want it, that's when you have truly grown to outgrow whatever that may be.

- ☀ Not wanting brings the happiness and freedom you are seeking in wanting.

> *Power-Quote: "The way to gain anything is to lose it."*
>
> **~Swami Rama Tirtha**

The Great Dane

An expected loss and an unexpected gain were coming. Bugsy, my white male boxer was old and sick. A tumor was discovered in his mouth near his throat. It was only a matter of time before he would be unable to swallow. When it was time, David said he would accompany me in putting my Bugsy down. This was David, hard on the outside and soft and loving on the inside. We both cried together, and it meant the world to me that he was there for me in both happy and sad situations. David got me through the heartache. The experience, although not so pleasant, once again bonded us even more. I was sad to lose my baby boy but knew it would be easier on David to have only one dog in our home. A huge surprise was around the corner...

BIG gestures were something David took pride in. On Mother's Day 2018, he told me he had a surprise that I could not have immediately. He said, "Don't get too excited, but my brother Carson has a friend whose dog had a litter of puppies." I knew what that meant and started jumping up and down in excitement. Just because I dropped the NEED to have dogs to be happy did not mean that I wasn't thrilled and overjoyed to be getting one! This was beyond unexpected and truly an act of love from my hubby. He nearly hated dogs but wanted me to have one because he knew how much I loved them. We were both looking forward to an adventure and new experience together in raising a puppy. Another win-win.

David didn't have a good feeling about the puppy's owners and how things were going down. He assured me that we would still get a puppy, just not that particular one. I let David be in the driver's seat and take the lead on the puppy search. Of course, I would be a part of all the decisions, but he was driving them. I remember this so well, he said, "I picked out the top four breeds; 1. Great Dane, 2...." I stopped him right when he uttered the words "Great Dane". THIS WAS MY DREAM DOG. I lived in California for a few years in my early twenties on Venice beach, while attending "Otis College of Art and Design". A Harlequin white and black spotted Great Dane would slowly walk by with his owner almost daily. I was in awe of this regal, gentle giant. Living in a studio and owning a Great Dane was an impossible idea.

The Great Dane puppy adventure began. This was a very thorough process for David in finding the perfect puppy. He did extensive research, as usual, to find us the most flawless pure breed, male, blue great dane. He picked the plumpest boy in the liter with an impeccable satin blue coat. The breeders were in Ohio. We agreed to meet halfway and pick him up. We had already gone through the name game with the first pup that we ended up not getting. Onyx was the most suitable name for our adorable new baby boy. He was spectacular, the biggest in the liter with bright blue eyes (that eventually turned green). This little ball of gray with GIANT paws and dumbo ears immediately stole our hearts. I was in HEAVEN. David sat in the backseat to bond with our baby in his arms on the drive back home. Onyx weighed a whopping eighteen pounds at only ten weeks old, which was short-lived!

Caren Paskel

The Power of Self-Belief

Power-Thought: Happiness Resides Inside

- ☀ When you start looking for happiness inside, you stop looking outside and everything comes to you!
- ☀ Chasing happiness is like a dog chasing its tail; running in circles only to find that you still have not found it.
- ☀ The endless external pursuit of acquisition and enjoyment causes stress, frustration, and displeasure.
    - ⊙ Joy is lost in your hunt to have and keep it.
- ☀ Nothing can rob you of your inherent happiness.
    - ⊙ No matter what comes or goes, your happiness remains.
- ☀ When you want what you have, you have everything you want!
- ☀ There's no need to get rid of all of your possessions or disallow acquisition!
    - ⊙ Throwing everything away or accumulating more won't make you happy.
- ☀ By locating your happiness inside yourself, you're putting an end to craving, desiring, and running after the world for happiness.

- ☀ The happiness living inside of you will gift you in many ways unexpectedly. You will be surprised what lands in your lap WITHOUT even wanting it. Now that's enjoyable!

- ☀ Once you realize your happiness is within you, the pursuit for happiness outside of you ends.

> *Power-Quote: "When you discover that all happiness is inside you, the wanting and needing are over and life gets very exciting."*

-Byron Katie

The Massive Seizure

When I stopped chasing love and loved myself, love came to me. Pre-David, I was desperately searching for my *Soulmate*. My desperate attempts failed. Once I began to trust myself and in Divine timing, a *Soulmate* appeared. This deep connection is beyond comprehension and words. I'll give my best in describing. It's an exchange of gifts. You are gifting another person with who you are, and they are gifting you with who they are. Together these gifts assist one another to further grow and progress. David and I complemented each other in exchanging our gifts. We were a perfect fit despite our twelve-year age difference, opposite upbringings, and distinct personalities! We were moving forward in our relationship and careers at a fast pace. It seemed as though nothing could stop us. But then something did, a massive seizure.

The honeymoon ended on Father's Day of 2018, just one year after our EPIC two-week wedding travel adventure in Italy and Switzerland. This was only two weeks after bringing baby Onyx home. He was fast asleep in his giant crate before the episode took place. David was entering from outside our home. He had grilled up some food after spending the day cleaning the entire house for me (very unusual for him) while I was at work. He wanted me to be able to relax when I got home. He went all out and even wrote me a little card. Thinking about this day brings me to tears every time. He told me that he did not feel right and felt weird. I said we would go to the ER after my shower if he still felt this way. It was a Sunday, and we would not be able to get ahold of our regular doctor. As I came downstairs, David was carrying in a platter of food from outside. His body began to tremor. I wasn't sure what was happening and thought it was some kind of joke. David was always messing with me. But he wasn't joking, he was seizing. I grabbed the platter and put it on the table.

He continued to have convulsions and fell to the floor, barely breathing and foaming from the mouth. His nose was bleeding too. My phone happened to be in my hand. I was able to ask Siri to call 911. Never having witnessed a person having a seizure, I thought that my husband was dying there and then. By the time EMS got to us, David was regaining consciousness. He wasn't aware of what happened, and I was in utter shock. He had experienced a grand-mal seizure. They took him to Henry Ford hospital and I followed right behind. I recall seeing Onyx in my periphery during the episode. He was pinned to the back of his crate shaking like a leaf. Onyx saw and heard my panic and fear talking with the 911 assistant, EMS entering our home with a stretcher, and then exiting our home.

At this time, my family was dealing with a lot. My sister's son was diagnosed with a rare genetic illness that affected his entire vascular system. My parents were on their way to Cleveland Clinic to support my sister and her family, for a very complex surgery that he would be undergoing. When I called my parents about David's seizure and being rushed to the ER they were already halfway to Cleveland and could not be there for me. The only person who lived nearby that I could think of was David's best friend Matt. He met me at the hospital. When I explained to him what went down, he looked at me and said, "Caren I think I know what this is. My mom had brain cancer". His mother did not only have brain cancer, but she also died of brain cancer. We had no information as to the cause of David's seizure. I disregarded Matt's words and tried to remain as calm and positive as possible. Once the scan showed a mass in his brain, my optimism began to wane. An MRI confirmed an orange-sized brain tumor. At that moment, everything changed.

A life-threatening illness did not scare or stop my husband. The brain tumor was David's wake-up call. His self-belief gave him the power to plow forward and live every moment as if it were his last. His drive and determination became even stronger. He used this devastating news to climb higher. He would not allow a tumor to ruin his life! It was my turn to step up with him, care for him, and serve him. It was time to take our relationship to a whole new level. *Soulmates* take on hardships together to lift one another and make the other even better. This is what happened to both of us.

Power-Thought: Find and Seek Hidden Blessings

- ☼ You have a choice in how you perceive life. You may choose to perceive challenges as opportunities to grow and learn. Or, you may not.
- ☼ Become aware of the innumerable blessings that exist.
  - ⊙ With this awareness, you develop a deep sense of gratitude and appreciation.
- ☼ Have X-ray vision to see through and extract the hidden gems that are there.
- ☼ By finding and seeking hidden blessings you do not fall prey to the victim mentality; believing that life is unfair and the world and everyone else is out to get you or to blame.
- ☼ Practice finding and seeking hidden blessings to embrace the so-called tragedies, difficulties, or conflicts rather than averting or avoiding them.
  - ⊙ You will overcome and rise above.
- ☼ By looking at a challenge as a chance to resolve and evolve you gain tremendous internal strength and resilience.

> *Power Quote: "When you find and seek the hidden blessings, the worst scenarios in life bring out the best in you."*

~Caren Paskel

The Housemate

The seemingly worst scenario brought a beautiful blessing into our lives. David's younger brother Daniel was part of David's team and worked with him in the Detroit office near our home. Before the massive seizure took place, David had proposed to me the idea of him moving in with us. An easier commute made sense. Daniel was introverted and his personality did not bother me. The old me would have said NO to living with anyone other than my husband and dogs. The new me agreed on him living with us. David was thrilled. He rarely thought highly of anyone, but he did so of Daniel. Daniel had all the traits of becoming super successful and David wanted to encourage him and help him be his best. Our decision opened up our homes and families to have the support, help, and love needed for a life-threatening event ahead. Daniel would be moving in much sooner rather than later.

Shortly after our conversation about the potential of Daniel being our housemate, David had his first seizure. Within days, Daniel moved into our loft, the size of a one-bedroom apartment or condo. David and I were grateful to have the helping hand of a family member. We had no idea how much Daniel would mean to us in sharing our home. Daniel and I became David's caregivers for the next two years of his illness until the very end and one year thereafter. We could have never predicted any of this. I don't know how I would have survived or gotten through without Daniel. Thank goodness I wasn't stuck in my stubbornness and accepted Daniel into our home with open arms. I got out of my way and trusted myself to do what was best for all of us, especially for David. A sacrifice was necessary for the greater good. In divine timing, Daniel landed in our home.

The Power of Self-Belief

Power-Thought: Trust Divine Timing

- ☀ Trust in Divine timing is an understanding that everything will unfold. Do what you ought to do when it ought to be done, whether you like it or not.

  - ⊙ In simple terms, do the right thing!

- ☀ Set the right direction for your life and follow that path.

- ☀ Learn by observing Mother Nature. She is pristine.

- ☀ You have a purpose and are a beautiful spoke in the Divine wheel of life.

- ☀ Play your part and allow everything to fall into place naturally!

  - ⊙ What's your part to play?

  - ⊙ What are your gifts and talents?

  - ⊙ Whom are you meant to serve?

  - ⊙ What are you meant to do?

- ☀ Trust yourself and the flow of life. Honor who you are and what you are meant to do here on earth. Otherwise, there will be resistance.

> *Power-Quote: "Trust in Divine timing… it's spiritual synchronicity. The alignment of people, places, and events choreographed for your soul's highest good."*

~Unknown Artist

The First Brain Tumor

Strangely, David's first brain tumor brought out the best in both of us and brought us closer together. We had to slow down and reevaluate our lives and that was a gift. The orange-sized brain tumor needed to be surgically removed without post-treatment, such as radiation or chemotherapy. Since he was already admitted to the hospital, they kept him there to monitor him before surgery. He was at the hospital for almost three weeks pre-and post-surgery. It was summertime and there was a huge outdoor courtyard. I asked if it was ok to bring puppy Onyx outside in the courtyard so that David could see his baby boy and get some fresh air. Each day I would bring Onyx to see his daddy. David rolled around with the plumpest little guy on the grass and held him in his wheelchair. It was quite difficult to make this happen daily. Onyx hated his crate in the car and would cry the entire time. He was also a huge puppy and not easy to transport. The joy brought to David was all worth it and allowed them to bond while he was in the hospital.

We made the most out of being in the hospital for so long. The husband of one of my yoga students was a wildlife photographer. He had reached out to me and asked to photograph Onyx for his portfolio. I thought this would be an ideal family photo opportunity! I shared what we were going through and asked if he would come to the hospital to take some pictures of Onyx, David, and me. He was more than happy to do so and captured the most beautiful and bright photos at a time that some might think was the darkest. The images of us did not show worry, pain, or tragedy. They revealed gratitude, strength, and love. One would never have known from the photoshoot that David was in the hospital about to undergo craniology surgery.

The first brain tumor wasn't a terminal diagnosis. We focused on the good news as David would not have it any other way. Immediately, David began working his butt off to ensure his health and life. He made drastic changes to his diet, exercise regime, and lifestyle. He believed he would beat the odds. The anti-seizure medications slowed his mind and body down, which led him to feel lethargic and irritated. There were plenty of other disabilities as well due to having gone through invasive brain surgery. Post-surgery, being more limited was his greatest frustration.

When we met, David's retention was off the charts. He stored all of his client's files in his memory with no paper trail. It was astounding to my scatterbrain! He did not have the same capacity after surgery. Having to rely on me and others was hard for him to accept. He was used to being able to do everything on his own. He was also the most resourceful person and a problem solver for everyone else. One thing didn't change. The power of self-belief pushed David to live fully and happily for the next year despite awful side effects and needing outside assistance.

David's determination kept him going. He was set on getting off his seizure meds. He worked hard to do this, and it was difficult to watch. I supported what he was determined to do for himself. For him, getting off the seizure meds was a step toward returning to his high-functioning self. And no matter how bad things got, he was going to try and try again. That's why he was successful. He never gave up. He weaned off slowly but ended up having another seizure. I was more prepared but still scared. He was in his office, and I was nearby. He said, "I think I am going to have a seizure". I said, "Ok honey, come sit on the couch so you are safe, I am here, and you are going to be ok". I called Daniel downstairs. Then it happened. I held him while he seized. It was unlike the first one, not as intense nor was he unconscious. I was beyond terrified for his life. Afterward, David insisted on not going to the hospital. Daniel and I were unequipped and wanted to ensure his safety. We went back to the hospital. They pumped him with seizure meds which was the opposite of what he was trying to do. He was pissed off but stabilized. We went home.

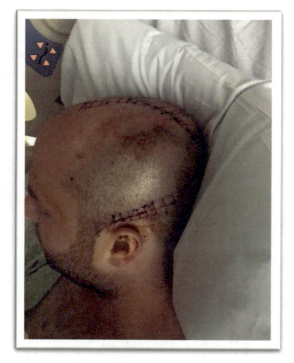

June 28, 2018

The Power of Self-Belief

Power-Thought: Determination Drives You Forward

- ☀ Determination is defined as the subtle faculty in a human that makes one strive consistently towards a goal. You will have the enthusiasm and courage to obtain your goals by confronting and overcoming all impediments.

- ☀ With determination, you can face all obstacles in your life. You will always keep going. A failed attempt will never stop you.

  - ⊙ Failure is one step closer to success.

- ☀ The determining factor in life is your willingness to persevere.

- ☀ Moving on to phase two, the next chapter, you will see there's nothing that kept David from being determined. He had the drive to move forward no matter what happened...

> *Power-Quote: "Determination is the wake-up call to the human will."*

> ~**Tony Robbins**

PHASE TWO

Overseas Overwhelm Plus Moving Madness

The Ireland Issues

David had the will to live LARGELY. Nothing and nobody, not even what his doctors advised, would keep him from doing so. He wanted to see and adventure the world. Only a few months after David's first surgery he insistently planned us a trip to Ireland where some business partners resided. Neither of us had been there before. We had an opportunity to play and explore mixed with a bit of business.

In the past, David did all of our planning. Traveling meant going along on David's ride. That was not the case for our Ireland excursion. He was unwell and erratic from going on and off his seizure meds. He was physically and mentally compromised. This was the first time in our relationship I had to do all of the things he would have been doing. I did the driving and navigating in a foreign country and the car drives on the opposite side of the street. I nearly killed us both multiple times. David's epic plan was to drive across the country of Ireland and visit historic relics, tour the oldest castles, and drink Guinness along the way at various taverns. The scenic route was incredible. What was not in the plan was ME driving us across the country. But I did it.

Looking back, it was as though this was all part of David's plan, to make Caren stronger and to believe that she could do anything. Well, it worked. I was forced to mentally toughen up, to a whole new level. There wasn't room or time for my old behaviors of complaining or whining. I had to handle being stressed from David's condition, having severe motion sickness, jet lag, and getting food poisoning in the middle of the trip. Yes, I was dry heaving on the bathroom floor over the toilet in our beautifully charming hotel suite. I stepped up, faced all issues, and figured it out for both of us. Believing in myself propelled me to do what was necessary.

 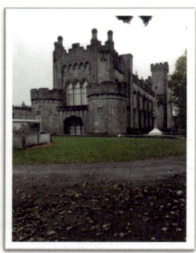

Power-Thought: Complaining Is Draining

- When you complain you drain yourself and those around you.
- Complaining drags, you and others down.
- When you learn how to express yourself without complaining you will not only help lift yourself and move forward, but you will also help others understand what you are going through, and how they may aid or support you.
- Complaining stunts your ability to find solutions to your problems.
- Complaints are a waste of your time and energy. They get you nowhere but stuck in the muck of whatever you are complaining about, with no way out!
- Check yourself before you wreck yourself. Stop your complaining and start dealing with and handling your life head-on.

The Power of Self-Belief

☀ If you are alive, there's nothing to complain about!

> *Power-Quote: "Never waste a second of your life complaining. Complaining doesn't solve problems, it attracts them. The more you complain, the more problems you'll have. And the more you infect other people with your problems. Don't be an infection. Be a cure."*

~Isaiah Hankel

The Missed MRI

David didn't complain about his failed attempt at going off his seizure meds or the day-to-day complications he was experiencing. He concentrated on living his life and planning our next venture. The first couple of David's MRIs came back better and better. To the doctors, it appeared that the little bit of tumor that could not be removed seemed to have vanished. What remained was more likely to be only scar tissue. The great news uplifted us, our families, friends, and co-workers. We thought this was the end of brain cancer.

Most sub-thirty-year-olds don't think of their mortality. David recognized that life was short and treated each day like it was his last. Even if he lived for a hundred years, he was not going to put off his dreams. Once we got back from Ireland, David started to plan our most EPIC five-week overseas adventure. We were going to stay in South Africa for the majority and explore a few days in Amsterdam and Paris on both ends of the trip. The timeline was less than one-year post-first surgery.

David was scheduled for an MRI every three months. MRIs were not a fun experience for either of us, especially him. He dreaded them. After his second seizure, I don't think he wanted to know if there was tumor growth causing his symptoms. The previous MRIs had shown so much improvement. Any mark of change, in the slightest negative, would put our upcoming excursion in jeopardy. He called his doctor to ask if he could postpone the upcoming scheduled MRI until after we got home. With a "yes", David canceled his MRI, and we flew away.

Caren Paskel

Shortly after arriving in South Africa, David experienced more severe symptoms such as losing feeling on the entire right side of his body. The cause was undetermined. Possible effects of travel, oncoming seizures, or tumor growth. Although we didn't know the cause, we knew it wasn't good. I suggested David go to the hospital and get an MRI in South Africa, but he would not. We would find out why soon enough. David chose to push through as far as he could go to fully enjoy our fantastically planned trip of a lifetime.

Power-Thought: You Become What You Focus On

- ☀ Where's your focus? Think about it. Whatever you have been focusing on you have become. Whatever you direct your focus to you will become.

- ☀ When you focus on something, you start to identify with whatever it may be, and you will therefore be affected by whatever that is.

    - ⊙ Anything that's out of focus is blurred, or in the background, and won't bother you.

    - ⊙ For example, if you focus solely on your career, you become so identified with what you do in your career that you become involved. Being so involved, you lose yourself. You work all the time. Even when you are not working, you are thinking about work. Whatever happens in your career, good or bad up or down will throw you around.

- ☀ Apply this concept of focus to your body, mind, intellect, significant other, children, family members, friends, politics, beliefs, religion, etc....

- ☀ Shift your focus to a lofty goal or ideal in life, that's not solely about or just for you, and everything below will not touch you. You won't be mentally disturbed and bothered by the mundane material changes and challenges of life.

☀ When your mind is set and focused on something above you grow and go towards that without getting sucked into worldly entanglements.

Power-Quote: "As you think, so shall you become."

-Bruce Lee

The South Africa Shift

The time had come for me to focus more on believing in myself and shift into high gear. David was unable to drive as the entire right side of his body wasn't working properly and undergoing regular seizure symptoms. Not only was the driver's seat and road on the opposite side, but I also had to learn how to drive a stick shift! David had to teach me, and I learned to do so up a narrow, windy road. This was beyond terrifying. I still don't know how I did this under pressure. Something else inside of me, took over. The power of my self-belief shifted me. I drove us everywhere with several near-death incidents.

David was most likely having mini seizures throughout the trip. When we got to wine country, things got bad, to the point of me having to call the hotel manager to our room. David was in bed curled up in a little ball shivering from head to toe. I was going into panic mode inside and hiding it on the outside, for both our sakes. The episode lasted about thirty to forty-five minutes. David did not want to miss anything and also felt bad for me. I reassured him that I was happy to stay in the room and order room service. But he wouldn't have it! He made me go to dinner and said he would meet me there. He arrived at the dinner table unwell. We returned to the room to carry out our evening and had an incredible date. He confided in me and said he was scared the tumor was growing back… I gave him options, to go home or visit the hospital where we were, and he did not like either. As he got worse and worse, we decided to shorten our trip. We still went to Paris, and we left South Africa a week earlier than planned.

Despite all the struggles and my terrible navigation skills, we managed to do everything we wanted together as the strongest team we had become. From Africa to France, we wined and dined daily, shopped, and explored museums and historic landmarks like the Eiffel Tower. We stayed in luxury five-star hotels and hiked up the most incredible mountain in Cape Town, *Lion's Head*. We drove through a national park and basically went on our own safari, which at one point had us surrounded by a herd of lions! While driving, I pissed off a black mamba by unknowingly clipping the end of its tail. When the snake rose above our car and hissed at our window, David jumped out of his seat and hit his head on the ceiling of the car! We visited the best wineries, had the most exquisite wine tours, and met the most interesting people along the way. I think David knew, deep down, that this could be his last chance for an unfathomable escapade. It was as though he was trying to squeeze all that he dreamed of doing into one trip. He wasn't going to allow anything to get in his way. And he didn't. He got to do it all. The role I played on this voyage shifted me. My confidence in my abilities to do anything skyrocketed. Being in the driver's seat, so to speak, proved I could do anything I set my mind to. Weak Caren, who always complained, and whom everyone else took care of, no longer existed. I took the bull by the horns.

The Power of Self-Belief

Caren Paskel

Power Thought: Self-Belief Conquers Self-Limiting Beliefs

- ☀ When you start believing in yourself, your self-limiting beliefs no longer hold power over you and your life. Take your power back!

- ☀ Self-belief is uniting with the higher power that's within you. This greater power overrides the lower self-limiting beliefs that impedes your growth and no longer serves your best self and best life.

- ☀ Self-belief gives you the competence to handle all of life's eventualities with grace and a smile on your face. You can conquer all that comes your way and swiftly bounce back from disastrous circumstances.

- ☀ Self-belief wipes out your self-limiting beliefs to regain your true inner power.

Power-Quote: "Buddha's teaching is that you are your own master; everything depends on yourself."

~Dalai Lama

The Moving Disaster

I was beginning to realize my self-belief was all I truly had to depend on. We were coming up to the two-year mark of living in our first home together on Parkside. And, just as David planned, despite his health condition and all that came with it, he was on the hunt for the next new home. I knew the timing of moving would be beyond stressful for both of us. But David was determined as hell. He had to follow through with his plan. It gave him purpose and something other than brain tumors, cancer, MRIs, seizures, medications, side effects, and fear of the unknown to focus on. Nobody could change his mind. The moving madness began.

We found an even bigger home more beautiful than the small castle we lived in on Parkside. It was a good investment that would take tons of renovating. We decided to go for it. The house on Cambridge Avenue was a medium-size castle with an adequate-sized backyard for our boy Onyx to frolic, play, and zoom around. David had extensive construction plans. And so it began. We started packing up our home. We were supposed to move into our new home before our South Africa travel extravaganza. That did not happen as the house was nowhere near ready.

Complete madness. The move-in date for the new owners of our Parkside home was set somewhere in the middle of our overseas travel. David would not change our travel dates, and I understood why. He had to keep living his dreams and he had to do it now. There was no other time. The realization for both of us, from his life-threatening diagnosis, was not to take one second of life for granted. The move happened while we were away. I let go of what might not make it to the second house, things that could break or be lost were unimportant. As long as my dogs survived.

What we came home to was a total disaster. But we knew that together we would find a way through. And we did.

Power-Thought: A Warrior Beats a Worrier

- ⚡ Worry comes from your mind. If you are unable to control your mind your worries take over and win. Worrying does nothing for you or anyone else but take you down and hold you back.

- ⚡ Your mind is what worries over your past and becomes anxious over your future. Most people spend the bulk of their life in a mental place of worry or angst. Mental disturbance impedes your ability to act.

- ⚡ Worrying does not help whatever you are worrying about, so there's no point in worrying about it.

- ⚡ When you aren't worried about the future you take the right actions in the present that move you forward.

- To beat your worries, you need a warrior intellect. A strong intellect beats your worries.

- Your intellect does not develop and becomes almighty on its own. YOU have to build it.

- The recipe to building your intellect is to start THINKING FOR YOURSELF at all times and stop following what others think, say, or do.

  - Don't simply take things for granted. Question everything!

  - When you exercise your thinking, you become a stronger thinker.

- Add your self-belief to your mighty intellect and you will become a true warrior of your life.

> *Power-Quote: "Worry is like a rocking chair: it gives you something to do, but it never gets you anywhere."*

> **~Erma Bombeck**

PHASE THREE

Holiday Hell Plus Deadly Diagnosis

The Homecoming Mayhem

David wasn't wasting time worrying. He was putting all of his energy into taking action on our new home when we returned from South Africa. His goal was to host Christmas at our new house. For David, Christmas was his favorite time of year. I loved this about him. All he wanted to do was gift everyone and mail handwritten cards to his co-workers, and there were a lot of them. He would spend an entire day wrapping presents with his mom so that every single child in his entire family, and there were a lot of those too, would get a gift from Uncle David. He loved making a Christmas statement. There were always surprises when we arrived at his mom's house. He was like Santa Claus! David was not only set on being home from our South African adventure for Christmas to celebrate with his family, but he was even more adamant about having Christmas at our Cambridge Avenue home. It was a good idea and would save us the lengthy drives to his family's homes, especially after our prolonged journey away and a homecoming with tons of unpacking ahead of us.

We had David's family and friends conduct the move while we were overseas. Describing the state of our new home, as being under construction, would be an understatement. The house was under FULL construction, with every room on all four stories. Upon arrival in the dead of winter, our homecoming was total mayhem. I remember this moment vividly. We opened the front door to a cloud of plaster and dust. Inside, it was freezing, and there was no hot water or working stove. There was a worker who looked up at us and said, "oh hey guys, welcome back, I thought you weren't arriving until next week". I was in disbelief and unable to utter a word besides gasping. I felt as though we were walking into a horrible nightmare. The tears began rolling down my face.

There were consequences to our choices and actions. Besides the home being unlivable and filthy with none of our belongings unpacked, my dogs were also in distress. Little Kylie was skin and bones. Somehow her feeding instructions got lost in communication with a family member appointed to care for the dogs. Everyone was on edge because of the crazy move and us not being there. Onyx was in a better state of health than Kylie, but he was beyond anxious with all the change and us being gone. My friend took both dogs in during the transition which was also disastrous. I pretty much broke down.

Power-Thought: Breakdowns Lead to Breakthroughs

- ☀ Sometimes life slams you with so much at once that it breaks you down. It's at those times that you must honor the low point that you are in, take care of yourself, whatever that means, and know that if you do so you will break through to the other side of your breakdown.

- ☀ If you are choosing to work on your self-development you will have support systems, proper teachings, and guidance in place to help you through. If you don't you won't! It will be way harder to break through if you even can.

- ☀ When are you able to lift yourself back up, slowly but surely, you will have come to an understanding of yourself and life that helps you navigate through what feels like disastrous times. You will be more prepared to handle life's occurrences.

Power-Quote: "When you have a breakdown, there's an opportunity for you to have an incredible breakthrough."

~Caren Paskel

The Power of Self-Belief

The Christmas Crisis

David chose not to break down. Brain cancer motivated him. He stuck his middle finger up to cancer and kept making big moves. That was my husband and that would not change. He stayed intent on hosting Christmas. I was a wreck, and a massive meltdown was brewing. Since we had no operational kitchen, I wasn't eating properly or taking good care of myself in the ways I needed to. My husband and my dog were extremely ill. The house was filled with construction workers hammering, sawing, and drilling daily. We had no privacy, and we were living out of boxes.

David was in a fury of action to get the house ready. He was in machine mode as if this would be his last one, and it was... As David and Daniel were slaving away on Christmas Eve Day, I was on my last leg. They wanted me to keep helping them, but I had nothing left. I tried and failed. David was getting upset with me. He was mad about the situation, but it came out on me. Daniel, having had to deal with the whole crisis also was highly stressed and that came out on me too. We were all exhausted, stressed out, and miserable, the recipe for a blow-up.

The Prentice's were bred to never stop doing and going. I grew up as a little princess who did not have to do much at all. If my bed was unmade my mom made it for me. If I was tired, I was encouraged to rest. I was picked up after and taken care of. The Prentice brothers were asking and expecting me to do hard labor that I wasn't built for. I remember the moment when I could not do one more thing and was crying about it. Daniel yelled at me, and I snapped. It was not his or anyone's fault. We were all operating in crisis mode.

The siren from within me went on. At my breaking point, I fled. All I can remember is getting in my car and driving to my parent's empty home, as they were in Florida at the time. Quivering from the inside out, I called my sister to help settle my nerves. I spent the next twenty-four hours in my parent's bed as a scared little girl. I believed in myself enough to know I needed the space to mend and pull myself together. To breathe air that was plaster and dust-free. To allow my body to be still instead of cleaning, moving, lifting, and running myself ragged. I needed a chance to cry, really hard and release all the stress from being out of the country with a sick husband with no family, friends, or doctors in reach. Saving my ass was the best choice for me and us even though I was absent on Christmas Day.

Power-Thought: Save Your Own Ass First

- ☀ There may not be a second ass to save if you don't save your own. You're the only one who can save yourself and that can be truly saved.

- ☀ The example of putting on an airplane oxygen mask yourself before helping another with theirs is an easy way to understand that if you run out of air, you cannot give someone else air!

- ☀ When you put everyone's needs before yours you become the one in need! You will go down in the process and take others down with you.

- ☀ Saving your own ass first means making sure you have the strength to carry on and care for or assist others.

- ☀ There's only one person you have control over and that is YOU! When you are out of control, do you think that is a good place to try and save or aid another individual? How helpful can you be when you require rescuing?

- ☀ When you choose to save your own ass first, it may appear you are being selfish to others. In taking care of yourself, you can give way more to others and truly be of service.

Power-Quote: "Nobody can save you but yourself - and you're worth saving. It's a war not easily won but if anything is worth winning - this is it."

~Charles Bukowski

The Reunion

Nobody could have saved me that Christmas other than myself. I would not have been a pleasant person to be around, to say the least. I was an emotional train wreck unable to contain my tears and fears. The time away was necessary for me to pull it together. When I came home, there was a cloud of tension in the air. What happened next was one of the deepest and most impactful experiences David and I shared in terms of our bond and the strength of the relationship. David felt abandoned. He came from a broken home as his parents separated when he was a young child. Although there was plenty of dysfunction in my home, my parents stayed together. There were open lines of communication to express our feelings to one another. Going to therapy was encouraged individually and as a unit. I don't know what David experienced growing up, only that it was different from mine. He thought that when I fled, it meant I was walking out on him and our marriage. On numerous occasions, I expressed to him that the only way he could get rid of me was by being unfaithful. But he was still skeptical.

David looked at me and said, "you didn't sign up for me being sick and if I were you, I would leave me too." I recall staring at him and standing there thinking, oh my God, he felt abandoned and thought I was going to leave him. My heart sunk and tears welled up. I lovingly reassured him, "baby, I married you because I love you in sickness and in health till death do us part. I am not leaving you ever. I needed to take care of myself because I was falling apart mentally and physically. Sometimes taking personal space to heal is necessary." I assured him that leaving the house was unlikely to happen again, but that in our marriage space was healthy, especially in really hard times, and would bring us even more together if we honored that. Without having this conversation, I'm not convinced that David would have fully trusted me to be by his side and to go through brain cancer every step of the way until his very end of life. Sometimes, the shit has to hit the fan to clear away the bullshit.

For the very first time, I saw David's self-belief become threatened by cancer. He felt like he wasn't good enough for me anymore, as if he were failing me because he was changing. It was a self-limiting belief that could not have been farther from the truth. I smashed that for him once and for all and ensured he knew I was not going anywhere. From this reunion, our relationship was sealed with a deeper trust and knowing that there was nothing that could break us apart. From the power of my self-belief, I was worthy of the self-care and space that brought us back together. For David, he was reassured that my love for him was pure.

Power-Thought: Allow for Breathing Room

- No matter whom you are in a relationship with, allowing for breathing room is necessary for individual growth and your relationship. If you are crowding someone or they crowd you, that will repel.

- Being on top of someone pushes them away eventually and leads to separation.

- For a healthy relationship, you need a lot of wiggle room to move around and be yourself! Otherwise, you will smother or be smothered. Not good!

- When you spend too much time with anyone, it will pull you apart. This is a law. Being miserable about being away from something or someone is an unhealthy feeling to have.

- If you're residing under the same roof as your partner or family members, there are ways of making room no matter how tight the living quarters are. For instance, you could simply go outside! Get creative in finding ways to make some room.

- You can only be happy in a relationship when you are happy with yourself. Dependency on others for your happiness will cause suffering.

- When you make room in your relationships you will enjoy them, and they will last. You will have the space to work, sort conflicts out, and resolve and solve your relationship issues.

☀ Room in relationships provides and keeps them fresh. It's good to miss your loved ones and keep that sense of missing.

> *Power-Quote: "Marriage is like a temple resting on two pillars. If they come too close to each other, the temple will collapse."*

~ Khalil Gibran

The Terminal Tumor

Thank goodness David and I permitted the breathing room for each of us to be in a rock-solid place to face what was brewing. After the Christmas crisis and before the New Year, David finally went in for the MRI that he had scheduled before our South Africa trip. The overdue MRI revealed another tumor that grew with a vengeance. It had a completely different name, glioblastoma, the deadliest kind of brain cancer. Immediate surgery was scheduled, and treatment was necessary. This was nothing in comparison to his first diagnosis. Glioblastoma is known to be lethal because the odds of living through treatment are slim to none. Did we wonder why we even get treatment with these odds? Yes, but David knew he might beat the odds and there was nothing to lose in trying. He was going to do everything he could to remain alive and fight like the boxer he once was who won the Golden Gloves. Nothing could stop or take away his determination to live. He believed he would be the one to survive. Self-belief allowed him to thrive and not merely survive for the remainder of his life. Through all the pain and decline he lived with an abundance of laughter, gratitude, and joy. He did what he could in every single moment until he couldn't.

David did not want to speak about death, nor would he allow me to be upset in front of him. I did my very best to cover up my sadness and fear of losing him. I cried a lot to myself and others. He was asking me to be strong for him to help him be stronger. Brain cancer was taking a massive toll on David. He was most discouraged by losing the cognitive functions that he depended on, identified with and most valued about himself. Pre-brain cancer, his retention, energy, ideas, and confidence were his prized possessions. Post brain cancer, I would whisper in his ear, "you are not your body or your brain, you are you no matter what you can or cannot do". He would look at me strangely. It would only be a matter of time before he could perhaps understand my attempt at instilling his power of self-belief despite losing the very things that he knew himself as. He had to learn that the true David was not how much he retained, built, or did. That he was more than all his functions and abilities. He resisted, but I never gave up because he would never give up on me. I became a positive person who believed in him when he was down, and in myself, for both of us.

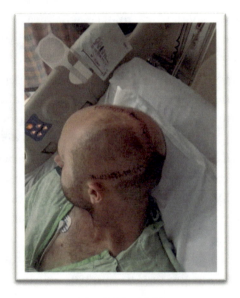

April 20, 2022

Power-Thought: Decide to Thrive

- ☼ Even with a death sentence or terminal diagnosis, you can either have a survivor or thriver mindset. The difference is self-belief. Without believing in yourself, you go into survival mode and are unable to enjoy any part of living.
- ☼ Survivors fight to stay alive while thrivers fight to be alive.
- ☼ A thriving mindset chooses to focus on being alive rather than the fear of dying.

- As a thriver, you never give up on your dreams even when you lose what's near and dear to you.

- You may go into survival mode without the self-belief to handle life. This is a coping mechanism for your protection. You will eventually burn out from this strategy.

- The power of self-belief shifts and lifts you into being a thriver. You can manage, learn and grow from every problem and alteration.

> *Power-Quote: "My mission in life is not merely to survive, but to thrive; and to do so with some passion, some compassion, some humor, and some style."*

~Maya Angelou

The Pancreatitis Scare

David and I kept our thriving mentality through more pain to come. The intensity of stressful situations all piled up one after another and landed me in the hospital. Leaving the house for Christmas for one day of self-care and rest was not nearly enough to recover. The breathing room was wonderful for our marriage but my body needed more attention and time to heal. I kept disregarding the various physical cues until the stabbing pain in the center of my abdomen was unbearable. For days prior I thought the pain was due to heartburn or acid reflux. To be honest, my physical irritation was the least of my concerns, considering my husband was going through radiation and chemo cycles and grappling daily with the loss of functions. I did what most caregivers tend to do, care for others and not myself to my detriment. I forgot to save my own ass first...

Before rushing out the door to an in-home client, my hands were holding the countertop as I pressed my hips back to relieve the immense discomfort. It had gotten worse and could not be put off any longer. I had a choice to disregard or regard the signals my body was giving. David and his best friend Matt were sitting at the table. I told them I was unwell and was going to take myself to Urgent Care. Neither of them knew how bad of a shape I was in and so I drove myself. From there I was sent to the ER as they did not have the proper equipment for a diagnosis. Being at the height of winter, everyone was sick, and the ER was packed. My sweet mother, the kindest soul on the planet, came to wait many hours and be by my side. God bless her. David's younger brother Daniel also came to the hospital. God bless him as well. That's how he was, he cared deeply for his family, and we are family now more than ever before.

At the hospital, they ran some tests and diagnosed me with Pancreatitis which means inflammation of the pancreas. How could this happen to me, a health-conscious yoga instructor who doesn't have a drinking problem? Stress can inflame any organ, that's how it happened. All the stress from traveling, navigating with a sick husband in a foreign country, and getting sick multiple times including heatstroke on our safari added up. Arriving home in a weakened state I got pummeled with more stress. Our home was under construction, we had no privacy, and on top of everything, David's car was stolen right in front of our home! If David was well, all of this would have been tolerated. But he wasn't so everything else became unbearable and my body suffered the consequences.

Being in the hospital for a few days forced me to heal and recover. They drugged me up and I slept most of the time. The pancreatitis scare was my wake-up call to take much better care of myself. Letting my health slide with everything going on was not ok, not for me or David. Not prioritizing my health could lead to more severe repercussions and being unable to care for my husband. From this point on my health became a high priority. I had suffered from health issues for most of my life. That's another book coming… My self-preservation was crucial to serving David. I formed a team of support for my health and made sure I saw them consistently. It was healing to have more ears to listen to and aid me in multiple ways.

The Power of Self-Belief

Power-Thought: Self-Preserve to Serve Others

- ☀ Think about what preserves food. Food preservatives lengthen a food's shelf life. YOU too can lengthen yours by self-preservation.

- ☀ Serve is in the word preserve. You cannot serve another without preserving yourself. This resembles saving your own ass first!

- ☀ Self-preservation is what you need to do to keep yourself up and in the best shape for your life! It looks different for everyone.

    - ⊙ What do you need to eat and how much?

    - ⊙ What type of exercise does your body need and how much?

    - ⊙ How much sleep do you need?

    - ⊙ What are you doing for emotional stability and the health of you mind?

    - ⊙ What are you doing to develop and keep your intellect sharp and maintain objectivity in life?

    - ⊙ What are you doing for your spiritual well-being, to connect with something greater than you?

- ☀ Self-care can be selfish when it's only about you and for you. Self-preservation is about keeping yourself up to SERVE your best self to all those around you.

- ☀ Self-preservation is the only way to truly be of service to others.

    - ⊙ Those who are best at preserving themselves are best at serving others.

Power-Quote: "The first law of nature is self-preservation. Cut that off, which may harm you. But if it is worth preserving and is meaningful, nourish it and have no regrets. Ultimately this is true living and love of self...from within."

~T.F. Hodge

PHASE FOUR

Pandemic Pivots Plus Top Brain Cancer Team

The Shut Down

We were doing our best to preserve ourselves. It was 2020. Our home was under construction, to no end. There was one problem after another, not only with the house but with David's health and both of our businesses. Treatment was not going well at all. And now there was a global pandemic, which heightened everything. In addition, my dog Kylie's health was diminishing, and her life was coming to an end. When David said, "Caren she's in pain", I knew it was time to say goodbye to my tiny rescue. Despite mostly disliking my dogs, David took a small fondness for Kylie during his illness. She kept him company. He used to want to "murder" her, in his words, when she incessantly whined for attention. One day I came downstairs to find David in his regular place at his computer sitting on his chair at the dining room table. Kylie was all curled up in a blanket on the chair next to him. David said, "she was crying so I made a spot for her next to me". He had that softer side to him that he rarely let anyone see that melted my heart. David loved me so much. Even while he could barely walk and was in horrible shape, he came to be with me to put Kylie down. We cried for many reasons. No matter his condition or state, he was always there for me. My tough man was the most loving and sensitive person, especially when I was hurting. Having him there meant the world to me. With him by my side, everything felt like it was going to be ok. I cherished that moment together.

After putting my sweet Kylie to rest, the shutdown mandates rolled in. Having a yoga studio was one of the worst businesses to own with the threat of a highly contagious airborne virus. I had to shut down my boutique yoga studio in Ferndale, MI. Without knowing how long this was going to be or what was going to happen in the future, my teachers and I used the studio space to live stream virtual yoga classes. This took a lot of pressure off me in one respect. With the bulk of my day-to-day management duties removed, there was more time to take care of myself and David. It was another blessing in disguise. At the studio, the change of scenery was fun and vital for my sanity. But something else much bigger was emerging inside of me.

Months went by with the studio being shut down. Students were dropping their memberships daily and revenue was plummeting at an alarming rate. Most of my teachers got tired of teaching online and had to figure out their lives too. This was painful to experience. Each client cancelation, or teacher leaving, felt like a hard punch in my gut. Fears of the yoga studios ending set in. However, there was an inner voice whispering that everything would fall into place and to trust myself. The whisper was the power of my self-belief that kept me going.

One morning, in our kitchen, David looked at me and said, "you need to make money". David's speech was limited. I knew what he meant, to figure out how to reinvent my business and move forward. He was right. Once again, at a very low point for him, the power of his self-belief inspired mine. Hours later I came across an incredibly informative webinar regarding how to grow your yoga business online. It was everything that I dreamed of doing but lacked the skills to do so, especially the technical ones that would enable the biggest business shift of my life. A call was booked and the largest investment in myself and my business thus far, with zero hesitation, was made! Immediately I got to work on the five-month personal and business development coaching program.

The Power of Self-Belief

Power-Thought: Closing Doors Opens New Ones

- ☀ It's true that when one door closes another one opens.

- ☀ When you try to keep a door open that needs to close, you sabotage your future openings.

- ☀ When you close the right doors at the right time, even if you don't want to or it's hard, there will always be a new one that opens you and your life in ways you never imagined or dreamed.

- ☀ Listen in to your deepest knowing and conviction. Stop trying to please everyone and abide by their wants and opinions.

- ☀ Take the time for deep reflection in the early hours of the day when the mind is most calm and the intellect most available to hear your truth. That truth will unlock your freedom.

> *Power-Quote: "When one door closes another door opens, we so often look so long and so regretfully upon the closed door that we do not see the ones which open for us."*

Alexander Graham Bell

The True Calling

Brain cancer opened the door to David's true calling. In 2018, post-first surgery, he reinvented his business. This was a HUGE switch that repositioned me as well. It was time to pivot and focus primarily on his health and our lives. He signed up for a thirty-thousand-dollar business development course with Grant Cardone. We supported each other's choices to grow ourselves and our businesses. We listened to many of the program lessons together. Although Grant's personality and language were geared towards David, my interest was piqued. David shifted his entire perspective and wanted to help teach people how to be happy, healthy, and successful in their careers. Having an enormous team, a business empire, and making billions of dollars was unimportant. He was compelled to work on himself and guide others on how to do the same to live their best life. Bigger was no longer better.

David loved teaching and it showed. At an entrepreneur event, he was a motivational speaker. He nailed the presentation and confidently engaged the crowd. His natural ability and confidence landed him a client. Working with and coaching her was a treasured time. He lit up while working with her. It was astounding to witness him find his true calling and prosper. From what others might have perceived as a setback, David turned into an opportunity to thrive even more and was overjoyed to inspire me.

One evening, I confided in David regarding tough business decisions. We were both very honest with one another. David was extremely good at expressing himself through writing. He sent me an email the very next morning with his afterthoughts:

Caren, last night was the best talk we've had in a long time in my opinion... I love seeing your passion come out! It seems we are on a similar life path to what we want to do to help people and I would love to see what we can come up with, as individuals and as a couple. Our empire and our legacy for our family. On the flip side, I don't like you stressing and not sleeping...

I have a gift for you that cost me thousands, but I firmly believe would see you to new heights. It's called 10x Stages. It's an 8-week course about building a business through speaking (on and offline stages). Each week there are a bunch of video modules and worksheets, followed by a longer coaching video to explain and answer questions. It's fucking brilliant. I'm using it and I think you could too to help a lot of people, be fulfilled with what you do, and make a lot of money doing it.

You may also benefit a lot from reading/watching some of Elena Cardone or Mel Robbin's content. It's really good and they've been successful at capturing huge audiences with messages I think you would agree with. Elena and Grant do collaborate at times which could be interesting. I can't think of another couple that does it.

Do yourself a favor and don't get caught up on the "How's"; focus on the "Why's" and "What's". I know how to do most of the "How's" and you can always learn from a program like this. Most people get overwhelmed with "How do I do that?" so I don't want you to get caught in that.

During the pandemic, the studio shut down and woke me up to my true calling. Owning a yoga studio was never my dream. It was one step on my path, a bridge to cross. I was compelled to mentally train more than physically and to Spiritually Educate full-time. Teaching ten plus yoga classes per week in addition to managing a yoga studio sucked my time. I did my best to find ways to honor my true calling. Pre-pandemic, I condensed the highest teachings from yoga philosophy into a weekend workshop called *CliffNotes on Happiness*. It was a success! The content came effortlessly and made for an abridged curriculum that would soon become my first online *Mental Training Course.*

David noticed how distracting it was for me to work from home. He suggested I use the studio. What a novel idea! "You are still paying rent, that's your office and you will get way more done," he remarked. Thereafter, I happily went off to work every day. In the blink of an eye, I launched *Mental Training Course 1.0; 11 CliffNotes on Happiness.* In less than thirty days, I signed up a lovely group of clients and grossed over twenty thousand dollars. David was beaming and so proud of my instant success. I had reinvented my business too. My true calling is Mental Training and Spiritual Education.

The bridge to my career potential was finally crossed. Viewing the power of self-belief in my husband catapulted me into my power. Self-belief elevated me to another plane of existence. David was lifted as well. He vicariously lived through my actions. When he was too unwell to coach and teach, I took the baton and started to fly. The power of self-belief carried us through the toughest times and kept our spirits up. Thank you, my dear husband David. Your self-belief gave me the power to keep going for both of us when you could no longer do so.

Caren Paskel

Power-Thought: Change Is a Wake-Up Call

- ☀ Rather than resisting change, let it wake you up! There's more to gain than lose from change if you see it that way. All you have to do is believe in yourself.

- ☀ Change is inevitable, so why resist? Allow change to shake you up in a good way that opens you up to your greater potential.

- ☀ Wanting things to stay the same is futile. First off, it's impossible. Secondly, there's no growth without change. Life would be so boring!

- ☀ Change means movement. Movement keeps you fresh. If you are not changing and moving, you are stagnating! More life breeds in rivers, lakes, and oceans versus puddles, swamps, and ponds. Keep things flowing, it will keep you alive and well!

  - ⊙ Staying open-minded and learning about yourself and life, through fluctuations, keeps you young!

- ☀ Welcome change, especially the drastic kind.

- ☀ Be grateful for your wake-up calls through the changes of life.

> *Power-Quote: "There is no growth without change. You've got to let go of some old stuff. And that can hurt. Often when I'm in the most pain, I realize it's coming from me trying to control everything. Or resisting the changes that come with the progress. But you see that light... that beautiful next level... & that's what you have to focus on.*

~Ali Brown

The Appointment

The time had come for a major change in thinking and treatment plans. David was rapidly declining while undergoing extensive radiation and chemo cycles post-second surgery. He wasn't getting any better. Our local doctors did not provide any other options. Giving up was never an option for David. We shifted gears. Researching on our own and with the help of my dad, we discovered the top brain cancer team and

The Power of Self-Belief

specialists in the world at Duke University in North Carolina. Fortunately, Dr. Henry Friedman took David on as a patient. We were no longer alone in our fight. We were in the best hands and ready for a new adventure. David believed in himself so much that he was willing to do whatever it took to stay alive, even if that meant traveling with brain cancer during a pandemic. His appointment at Duke was made and our travel plans were booked.

The first flight was a fiasco and shook us to our core. We made it to the airport and the flight was delayed. David had immense brain swelling and was struggling to sit upright waiting hours for the next available flight. The good news was that the airport was a ghost town. We upgraded our seats as the flight was empty and our situation was obvious. David was nodding in and out on the plane. He barely made it through traveling. Watching his symptoms escalate, I felt anxious and scared as to the shape he was in. Making it to our destination was surely his self-belief.

We stayed at a beautiful hotel on the golf course minutes away from the University. It was gorgeous. David was one of the few non-local patients allowed to stay at the hotel. Upon our arrival, David's state accelerated. He had a horrible headache. We tried ordering some food and sitting outside. Within minutes we had to retreat to our room. Our first appointment with Dr. Friedman and his team was the next morning. David was ever-determined to make it there. His body was uncooperative. What happened next was one of the more terrifying episodes for both of us. His headache was unbearable, and he fully lost his speech. I called the hotel emergency line and EMS shortly arrived. I was the communicator, as David could only shake his head yes and no. Because of the state of the world, they would not allow me to go with him to the ER. This might have been the most upsetting moment of my life. I felt complete and utter helplessness and despair for what my husband was going through and there was nothing I could do about it or be with him. The panic set in when they rolled him out of our room and took him away from me. I phoned my brother. It was the middle of the night as he was in Pacific Standard Time. He picked up, thank

Caren Paskel

goodness, and helped me breathe again so I could stay centered while the unknown was happening to my husband.

Nurses and Doctors from the ER called me for communication all through the night. I do not know what they gave him or did to him. My strong-willed husband was not going to miss his appointment that morning. The power of self-belief gives an inner strength that is stronger than any other force. Hours later, somehow and some way I received a text from him that he was on his way back. He left the ER on his own, stood outside by himself, and figured out how to get a Lyft back to the hotel! Unbelievable… He was back with me in my arms safe and sound. The nightmare seemed to have ended, at least for that moment, and nothing else mattered.

It was a miracle that we made it to our morning appointment with Dr. Friedman and his team. Beyond being exhausted and resembling zombies we finally got to the finish line. We felt immense relief on the inside and showed tears on the outside. Dr. Friedman's team came to the rescue. That very day he was put on a drug that reduced his swelling dramatically. Within hours he was talking and walking. The head oncologist in Detroit made fun of Dr. Friedman's so-called model of selling HOPE to his patients and their families. David and I agreed that hope sounded wonderful to us, and we were happy to have as much as possible. Hope was an upgrade to hopelessness and there were no other options. With our hopes up, the walls came down and we could focus on life, not death. The plan was to visit Duke every couple of months to stay on top of everything. We also went to a local facility at home for a drug infusion to keep David's swelling down. Things got a lot better for a small window of time.

The appointment changed everything for us. The way we were treated made us feel supported and loved. Their expertise was calming. We needed that more than words can relay. The appointment also gave us a plan and something to do rather than just wait for David to die. We concentrated on what we could do and not what we could not do. For David and me, it gave us more quality time together traveling, even though it was not for a fun reason. The change of scenery was

58

refreshing during the pandemic and got us away from the day-to-day. It was sort of a mini vacation especially when the hotel restaurants opened up! David and I went all out. We got a huge double room suite since nobody was in the hotel and dined like kings and queens. We celebrated, treated ourselves, and in return got the royal treatment.

Power-Thought: Perseverance Provides Inner Vigor

- ☼ When you tap into your self-belief you are tapping into a great force from within to persevere. You won't have the inner strength to persevere when you stop believing in yourself.

- ☼ Perseverance may get you through some of the most difficult times of your life in ways most are unable to. The very life and world challenges and changes that affect the majority won't affect one who possesses perseverance.

- ☼ Perseverance is an unwillingness to give up. There is no throwing in the towel EVER! You must try again and again to persevere.

- ☼ A perseverant attitude keeps you going and provides the inner vigor to do so.

> *Power-Quote: "Going on one more round, when you don't think you can, that's what makes all the difference."*

-Sylvester Stallone

The Pandemic Peeves

The more challenges that came David's way, the more he persevered. The pandemic pissed him off in a good way. He carried an attitude of "bring it on". He was fired up and dumbfounded by the world's reaction and response to a crisis. He believed that a fear-based reaction made everything worse. David was one of the most rational human beings that I had ever come across, which was one of the main reasons I married him. And, of course, he was NOT a rule follower. World, state restrictions, and mandates caused double the irritation with his various limitations due to brain cancer. Our contractors slowed down. Some of them even stopped right in the middle of working on the house. Our landscapers disappeared halfway through their job. David was beyond peeved and would not accept this. All the pandemic pangs motivated him to become more insistent to persevere and find other ways to get things done. Finishing the house gave David purpose even though it was a nightmare to encounter.

Masks also irked David. He was struggling physically and disabled. On top of being highly uncomfortable with his bodily functions and already feeling like crap, having to wear a mask heightened his physical discomfort and agitation. For David, terminal brain cancer trumped a virus. He wasn't going to allow anything worldly to get in the way of his life or stop him. Being peeved amplified David's toughness. We decided to rise above worldly chaos. We chose to become more resourceful and became more resilient. We found perks of the pandemic despite the entire world's unfortunate situation.

Power-Thought: Become Evolved and Not Involved

- Are you getting involved?
    - Do you lose sleep over things that happened in the past or may happen in the future?
    - Do you experience upset in your relationships?
    - Are you bothered by worldly affairs?
    - Do you get agitated by those who think differently than you?
    - Do you find it hard to mind your own business?
    - Do you take things personally?
    - Do you avoid certain people you are close with because of opposing views, beliefs, or personalities?
- It's impossible to be at peace when you are more involved than evolved. Getting involved impedes your evolution.

The Power of Self-Belief

- ☀ There is a way to be part of the world and not get caught up in its fluctuations.
  - ⊙ You can have close relationships without entanglement.
  - ⊙ You can do your work and not take it home with you (even if you work from home).
- ☀ When you focus on your self-development and the purpose of your existence, which is to grow into your greatest highest Self, you won't get dragged around by everyone and everything that's going on in your life and around you.
- ☀ Working to evolve turns you from material to spiritual.
- ☀ Evolving develops every part of you including your voice of reason. That is your intellect.
  - ⊙ A well-developed intellect breeds objectivity! Therefore, you are able to step back and observe from a different vantage point. You begin to recognize the 'show called life'.
- ☀ In becoming evolved you become entertained by life's display versus getting wrapped up in the drama.
- ☀ Clinging on will only pull you down and suck you in.
- ☀ The ride of your evolution elevates you and takes you above all that's happening beneath.

> *Power-Quote: "Worldly entanglement gets you wrapped up in chaos rather than unwrapping your inner peace".*

~Caren Paskel

The Good Results

David and I chose to evolve rather than get involved in the chaotic world. Our next visit to North Carolina was completely and drastically opposed to the first one. The memory makes me smile. We finally got to have some real fun at the hotel. In-house dining was open! Since David was able to walk, we took slow walks on the incredible hiking trail that went for miles around the hotel and campus. David was scheduled for his MRI the night before our appointment to discuss the results. The waiting period was always unsettling. David was feeling so much better and we were very confident to hear good results. The MRI from our last visit to this one vastly improved. The amazing news brought us tears of joy in the presence of Dr. Friedman and Nurse Rosemary.

Nurse Rosemary was the most incredible woman. God bless her heart and soul. She went above and beyond in her service to David and me. She gave us her cell phone number so that we could call or text her anytime. David communicated with her regularly. I took her up on the offer as well. She was our lifeline. Her sense of humor, zest for life, knowledge, and compassion was crucial for us. We fell in love with her. She was a saint that got David and me through some of the most grueling times and moments. She lifted us both up and was always positive. She was able to provide information and tools necessary for our survival. She made phone calls for us to the local in-state doctors we had to deal with, got us scripts, and went to any length for us to get what we needed when we needed it. She became family.

That evening, we had the best date night. We informed all our families of the great news, and everyone was relieved and happy! We were elated returning home. David was doing everything on his end to stay in good health. He even started running. He made a goal to run a 5k. Being unable to use or feel the right side of his body most of the time didn't divert his running goal. The power of self-belief gave him the ability to go beyond what anyone else thought or believed he could do. With consistent training and hard work, he was running! David was able to run two brain cancer 5k runs. It was his self-belief that crossed the finish line. Unfortunately, he did not make the last goal of running a third 5k, as his entire body failed him. But, his mind never gave up and that's how David lived until the end.

Power-Thought: Goals for Your Expansion

- ☀ You can make huge goals that nobody else believes are attainable with self-belief.
- ☀ When you expand your thinking, you will grow!
- ☀ Think bigger and broader than only about yourself.
    - ⊙ How far can you reach beyond your selfish interest?
- ☀ It's not about what you are going to get but rather what you are going to give. Worrying about yourself and what is going to happen to you is the root cause of your anxiety and stress!

- Your evolution makes an impact. What kind of impact depends on how much you're willing to extend yourself. The higher you climb spiritually, the more your expansion influences others. Your self-development is what you are giving to the world. Why would you keep that for only you, your family, or your community? Why not spread as far and wide as possible?
- Stretch yourself further and further in your goal of giving your best self to the world. You become more peaceful and happier the wider you go and grow.
- Mahatma Gandhi's famous quote, "Be the change you want to see in the world", means that your goal for your evolution is what impacts the world the most.

Power-Quote: *"The world is merely a reflection of each one's evolution."*

~Caren Paskel

PHASE FIVE

Roles Reversed Plus Endings

The Revival

Expanding on how to best serve my sick and dying husband had the greatest impact on both of us. The high we were on from the good MRI results fizzled. David was struggling with his meds. We were unaware his tumor was growing back. He would go up and mostly down. He would have some good moments, even days, followed by many more bad ones. He couldn't move the right side of his body and his speech was impaired. We hoped the complications were due to what seemed like an endless pursuit to ween off steroids. Unfortunately, brain cancer was coming back vehemently.

Unable to read or write David's self-belief began to wane. These were amongst the main qualities and assets David identified with the most: reading, retaining, applying, and incessantly writing. I have PILES of his books, boxes upon boxes, that he read and noted. He had journals of all his thoughts, ideas, and plans. He was always jotting things down. There were notes all over the house. He used his phone when there was no paper. When he lost those specific abilities, he felt useless. David loved to read, write and work. He felt utterly incapable. As he stood in our kitchen leaning on the countertop, I asked him what he was thinking about and he said, "nothing much, I don't have many thoughts anymore". Hearing him say that was heartbreaking.

Because David's right foot and leg were numb, he took some bad falls. He fell down our entire staircase multiple times. He was all bruised up and I was scared for his safety in our home. My strong, healthy, independent man was physically weak and dependent. His frustration finally got to him in a way that I had never witnessed before. He was lying face down in our bed with darkness around him. The shades were drawn, and he seemed lifeless and very still. He was at his lowest mental state. David's power of self-belief needed to be revived. I held myself back from any negative unproductive thoughts. My self-belief kicked in and took over. Believing in myself and serving him was the only thing that could shake and wake him back up. I wanted to help him live fully no matter what he could or could not do and to find purpose in every second of his existence. He uttered repeatedly "I can't do anything". My reply to him was, "yes you can. You are here now; you are alive and you have a purpose". David never wanted to be consoled, he wanted to be motivated, that was his role with everyone else. Our roles had reversed.

David was the first person to tell me to stop grumbling and go do the very thing, whatever it was, that I did not want to do. That's how I got stronger and was able to believe in myself. He woke me up in a way nobody else could or would. He didn't care how I felt by saying what I needed to hear. David was happy to point out regularly that being taken care of all of the time was not a good thing for me. Every time he did, I would stop dead in my tracks, eyes popping, jaw-dropping, and think, "holy crap, he's right". Then, I would thank him. Why the heck didn't anyone tell me about this vital information before? I had been to countless therapists, and not one of them ever suggested to stop whining, be an adult, and go figure it out! This was the GREATEST GIFT anyone handed me. There was no way I would ever be able to believe in myself without that awareness and advice. If that's what anyone reading my story needs to hear, "you're welcome" as David would say to me with a smirk;). David focused on winning and never whined.

Power-Thought: Be A Winner Not a Whiner

- Just as complaining is draining, whining is self-depleting. Whining sucks the energy, creativity, and constructive thinking right out of you. Whereas, winning refuels and fires you up.

- Self-Experiment: for 24 hours fixate on what you DO have and what you CAN do rather than what you don't have and what you can't do. After twenty-four hours without whining, while filling your cup with gratitude and positive thoughts, write down how you feel.

  - What was your experience talking with others?
  - Did they respond to you differently?
  - Note if you did this for one day and then try it for two days. Keep it going, why stop there?!

- Whining blocks you from winning. You lose your ability to problem-solve.

- Choosing to acknowledge your wins keeps you winning and builds the stamina and momentum for you to progress and flourish.

> *Power-Quote: "When you focus on your WINS every day and celebrate them, you will never lose."*

~Caren Paskel

The Spark

In the darkest hours of mental despair, winning over whining was the only way to go. I knew exactly what my husband needed to hear and how to say it. He already had an outline and content completed for his book. In a stern but loving tone I spoke to him, "David, it's not going to do you any good to focus on what you cannot do. Even though you may not be able to do the things you want in the way you want to do them, you can get your book finished and published." My belief in him restored his power. The spark of self-belief rekindled David's. His mission was for his book to be written and published. He was back in action the very next day.

David cared deeply about his legacy. Making a positive impact on other lives even after his life was over was of utmost importance. He was always thinking about what he was going to leave behind. That made him feel so alive. Finishing his book and getting it out there gave him peace knowing his life meant something. For him, that's what gave him purpose and solace until his end. On the contrary, I had no desire to write a book and never thought about what I was going to be leaving behind. David's self-belief gave me the courage to think beyond my preference. He was no longer here, but I was, so what could I do with that? Again, thank you, David, for leaving me with the power of self-belief and promise to bestow the invaluable, remarkable, and transformational message of self-belief to the masses.

David's resourcefulness had returned. He reached out to his dear friend and personal trainer. Josh was highly intelligent and had many talents beyond his expertise in physical fitness and functional training. Amongst his many trades, he was a published author! Josh was also David's friend. He came over to our home to conduct weekly personal training sessions with David. He trained David to relearn to use his right side, walk and even run. Josh would say, "David are you sure you want to run when you can hardly walk?" David would confidently reply, "yes and I know you are the person who can teach me and show me how". Even Josh was astounded by David's determination and fortitude. It was surely David's self-belief that pushed him to do all the various exercises he was assigned, multiple times a day. He was able to RUN with no feeling on his right side. Seeing this happen was incredible for Josh and me.

When David got off the phone with Josh that day, his eyes were bright and filled with excitement and zest for life. He could not wait to tell me that Josh jumped on an opportunity to assist with his book. David could not have been more thrilled to have his buddy help him finish and get his book out there. They got to work immediately! They sat at our beautiful dining room table that my mother had gotten for us

The Power of Self-Belief

as our housewarming gift before the crazy Christmas debacle. At the time, David could talk but not write. Josh conducted an interview style with David for writing. While making lunch, I'd be listening in the background. Sometimes, they would ask me questions in regard to timeline, get my take or figure something out that was hard for David to remember. The experience filled our home with joy. It was both positive and fun for all of us. The refocus gave David repurpose. David and Josh's collaboration lead to the publication and release of *Can't Doesn't Exist,* a number one bestseller on Amazon in both cancer and motivational/self-help categories!

Power-Thought: Self-Limiting Beliefs Breed Limitations

- ☀ Self-limiting beliefs limit YOU.

- ☀ It's interesting how most people update everything in their life from homes, wardrobes, and cars to all the technology. But, when it comes to beliefs, the majority won't take the time to update.

- ☀ You may be sitting on self-limiting beliefs that are limiting you in your life.

- ☀ Start by going through your core beliefs first. Core beliefs are usually your musts, shoulds, rules and demands. Check each one and see if they are limiting you in any way. If so, UPDATE them.

- ☀ When you begin to believe in yourself, that power enables you to update your old self-limiting beliefs and reach your limitless light source within. Your new and improved beliefs empower, drive you forward, and uplift those around you.

> *Power-Quote: "Your self-limiting beliefs never let you see a new outlook. So, keep these negative beliefs away and challenge them every day to change your perspective towards yourself as well as the world around you."*

> **~Ruchi Bali**

The Studio Closing

Believing in myself provided a fresh new outlook for my business during the pandemic. My yoga studio, *EnSoul Yoga*, located in the heart of downtown Ferndale, Michigan, was shut down for over seven months. Losing nearly 75% of clientele and revenue while still paying rent, I had to make a decision. My business accounts were being drained and the release of shutdown restrictions and mandates were unknown and uncertain. There was no end in sight. At this point, David was able to communicate and was always honest with me, even if I did not want to hear it, which I very much appreciated. He also supported what I wanted to do, even if it was not what he thought was best for me. In this case, he was most objective and recommended I close the studio for many obvious reasons. Mostly he was trying to protect my sanity in having a very sick husband. More obvious were the business-related problems of owning a yoga studio during a pandemic caused by an airborne virus. I took the steps my husband suggested. Sitting at our beautiful dining room table with David, his brother Daniel, and a couple of his closest friends, we deliberated. I could not have done this on my own with everything going on. Emotions surrounding my business, the studio, and the community were clouding my judgment. Clarity came from the group council. It was the right time to close the studio doors.

I thought long and hard about my mission and what was most important. Did I need a yoga studio to keep teaching and educating Spiritually? Nope. The power of self-belief opened my mind up to make a much bigger impact than a yoga studio could. The studio was limiting my ability to expand. What if I could share this knowledge of self-development in a universally practical and accessible way without being tied down to a location? From there it was easier to let go. I wasn't giving anything up, I was taking up something much greater and growing! This was one of the best decisions I ever made. Owning a small business, while learning a ton, became my entire life. Being on call 24/7 and managing most everyone and everything. With each manager hired, my income was considerably reduced and still did not give me a break! It was exhausting and took up all my energy and time...

The chapter of owning a studio location came to an end. I had more time to spend with and care for my husband without the stress of managing a studio. A new chapter of remote Mental Training and Spiritual Education began. My business expanded almost immediately. I doubled my revenue in one month. David got to watch me. He was blown away by what I was creating and building. His self-belief ignited my self-belief. The power of self-belief had me climbing to higher heights and gave me the strength to keep living through David's end. Sharing self-belief empowered and enriched both of us.

Power-Thought: Staying Small Stunts Your Growth

- Reasons why you may be staying small:
    - Don't have to push yourself
    - Don't have to be at your edge
    - Staying the same is more comfortable and safer
    - Past or present bullying or abuse
    - Scared of the unknown
    - Growth hurts
    - Fears, doubts, and insecurities
    - Lack of self-belief
    - Fear of failure and or success
    - Low self-worth and value
    - It's a good excuse to avoid what you do not like or want to do
- Problems with staying small:
    - Stunts your growth and self-development
    - Stunts your capacity to serve
    - Impossible to move forward

- ☉ Blinds you from seeing opportunities and others from seeing you

- ☼ SHOW UP in your vulnerability and with your imperfections. BE YOURSELF in all your glory with no apologies. What's the point of covering up and being fake?

- ☼ Open up and be seen! There's so much more to GIVE, receive and unite with. You cannot get there with small thinking and goals.

- ☼ You only shine when you believe you are worthy and divine.

> *Power-Quote: "Staying small is a disservice to humanity. Your ego need not grow, only your ability to serve."*

~Caren Paskel

The Last Birthday

Small was no longer an option. I wanted to go all out in celebrating David's BIG thirtieth birthday. In February 2020, chemo cycles were taking a heavy toll on my husband. He was having an excruciating time weaning off of his seizure meds. His body was becoming increasingly weaker, and he fell more frequently. Not sure how he survived falling down our wooden staircase. He was still a beast of a man. Many cognitive functions were diminishing as well. We called Nurse Rosemary, daily. I cried a lot, never in front of David as that would break his heart. When he fell, I felt as though I fell with him. It was harder to focus on the positive while watching him get frightfully worse and not better.

My father asked me a question on one of our phone calls while I was sobbing. "Is David still there? What I mean to ask you is that many who suffer from this form of brain cancer have drastic personality changes. Has David's personality changed?" The answer was a solid "NO"! My dad reminded me that David was still the stubborn, feisty, determined, slightly overconfident, strong-willed man he always was. Despite very few moments of despair and frustration, and being unable

The Power of Self-Belief

to do what he wanted, he was the same David that I married. What changed was his abilities and thankfully not his personality or nature. The new awareness that was brought to my attention converted anguish into gratefulness. My father gently helped me to realize a blessing disguised by fear, sadness, and pain.

February 24, was David's birthdate. He was alive and turning thirty. This was a HUGE birthday, not because he was the big three- O, but more importantly, it most likely would be his very last birthday in his physical form. David and my appreciation for each day of life grew tenfold. It would have been a shame to wait until it was too late. We were cognizant of the blessings and how brain cancer reshaped us and our lives. I know that might be an astonishing statement to read. Allow me to clarify. It's easy to get caught up in the day-to-day and lose sight of the purpose and meaning of life. David and I got to see the magic in every moment we had on our journey and together as one. The grandest gift gained from his life and the imprint he left was being fully conscious, utterly grateful, and undeniably appreciative at all times, especially amidst the chaos, loss, and suffering.

Some family members did not want to celebrate his thirtieth in the way we wanted to. I understand why. It was hard to see David feeling unwell and his end looming. He was sickly and everyone was concerned for his well-being. David wanted to keep living. If he was able to get dressed, make it into the car and go out to celebrate his life, that's what we were doing!

David was a people person, and it brought him joy, energy, and laughter to be amongst people, particularly friends and family. I invited his closest friends and immediate family to our spot, *Bistro Joe's*. We reserved the Chef's table to accommodate everyone. Although he wasn't at his best, he was still standing, smiling and happy to be celebrating his 30th with those he loved. Everyone said and gave meaningful words and presents. We had a party, while he was alive to celebrate his ability to thrive. He was a superman who deserved to be honored in the way that made him happy. I pushed so hard to make this happen, with pushback from others and it was worth it. Looking back, this was my newfound self-belief, the kind that David always had and could no longer express.

Power-Thought: The Greatest Gift Is Life

- Each day you wake up is a gift. When you open your eyes, you are opening the greatest present. The gift of being alive is to be celebrated every day!
- What's the first thing you do each day? Do your thoughts and actions honor the greatest gift you have been given?
    - Checking your phone, messages, and alerts
    - Watching the news or getting on social media
    - Getting dressed and out the door
    - Putting stimulants into your body

The Power of Self-Belief

- ☀ What if you recognized the gift of waking up, that not everyone received? You get another day, another chance to be out there and be you!

- ☀ When you celebrate awakening each day you rise above the B.S. Whatever is going on in your life or the world, won't bring you down.

- ☀ Here's how to put it into action:

  - ⊙ Acknowledge waking up is the greatest gift. If you open your eyes and can see, celebrate your eyesight! Same with all of your senses.

  - ⊙ Hooray, I can hear, smell, taste, and feel… If you wake up, be aware of that!

  - ⊙ Put your mind to something higher: Spiritual knowledge, words, and Eternal values that hold UNIVERSAL TRUTHS. Reflect, make them your own and work to apply them to your own life.

- ☀ Self-reflection is most effective in the earliest hours of the day to set your mind right for the changes and challenges you come across.

  - ⊙ Think about the 4 Am - 6 Am time slot. This may sound repulsive, slightly insane, and even impossible. BUT Mother Nature is the quietest and most peaceful at that time. So too is your mind. It's a law.

  - ⊙ When your mind is calm and clear, read and reflect on this book. You will get way more out of it. If you already read it, take the time to re-read it in the morning and you will have a different experience. You will be studying 80% and reading 20%. That's how to absorb and assimilate the teachings!

  - ⊙ Contemplation on TRUE knowledge builds and develops intellect, your reasoning faculty. When the intellect is strong you don't fall prey to your whims and fancies, emotions, and impulses of the mind. You become a master of your mind and not a slave. When you are in control of your mind you are in control of your life!

Power-Quote: "The mind is its own place, and in itself can make a heaven of hell, a hell of heaven."

-John Milton.

PHASE SIX

Family Dynamics Plus House of Gathering

The Families

My mind's preferences were challenged by distinct family dynamics. I was more of a loner and homebody. David was not. Our upbringings were dissimilar as well. David's family was huge compared to mine. His parents divorced when he was a child, and the two separate families grew. He had a brother and sister from the same parents, two half-brothers, and many step-siblings. He moved around a lot and lived in different homes. This is one of the reasons David was so adaptable! He could live anywhere and be ok. Plus, he was the oldest child while I was the youngest. Being a baby, I was not so adaptable. I grew up in a family of five with my parents and two older siblings. My parents are still together to this day, fifty-some years later, and live in the same house I grew up in. I have four nieces and two nephews. So far, that's as big as my immediate family extends.

When David and I met we became our own family and we had to split our time with his and mine for the holidays. We loved our families dearly. With traveling, opening up, and running our businesses we had very little spare time. Our life was FULL, and we were having a blast building our incredible relationship and life together. When David got sick, all of our families wanted to help support and be around a lot more. I was overwhelmed. My husband's illness, our home space, and our privacy were out of my control. I loved everyone and wanted David to be cared for and surrounded by his loved ones. This was an energetic tug of war for me. I had to dig so deep inside to figure out how to help myself through. I had to adapt to the circumstances and embrace the

Caren Paskel

influx of family members. I had to be prepared for regular unannounced or short notice drop-ins.

We both surrendered to family members showing up at our home daily. Most of the time David was happy about these visits. Sometimes he was unwell or not up to it. The family was unaware of how their timing of coming over might affect us. And that's ok, I knew everyone could see that David was dying and felt desperate to help in some way and to be around him. We were all very much aware that each day could be David's last, and everyone wanted to spend every second they could with him. I don't blame them, because I felt the same way. I did my best to adjust myself accordingly to accept and embrace what was happening. Yes, I had my moments of agitation and upset. Once I noticed what everyone was bringing to our home and to David, that filled me up with joy.

David's dad, stopped by the house for brief early morning visits, like clockwork. He would touch base with his son and have some laughs. He often dropped off mason jars of healthy homemade food and soup that his wife, David's stepmom made for him. On occasion, she would come to the house to give David a much-needed massage. David's mom, who lived about an hour away, came by more often as well. She would bring her best for David to see, ensuring that her son saw that she was doing good and staying strong. David's slightly younger sister came by as much as she could. Sometimes she would bring her two young boys, David's nephews, to help care for him. All she wanted to do was take care of David. She adored him and slept over some nights when things got really bad, to be there for him when he awoke. She was the first to observe that Daniel and I were unequipped in caring for David on our own. This was a horrible moment for Daniel and me. As much relief as it gave us to have professional help, it meant David was close to his end. David's other two brothers came over for visits and sometimes stayed overnight. David's step-sisters also came by to cheer up David. Each family member brought so much love, laughter, and cheer.

78

The Power of Self-Belief

Power-Thought: Adapting and Adjusting Is a Skill

- Change is an inevitable fact of life. When you can adapt and adjust, you can handle change.

- Those who are resistant to change, expecting that the world and others cater to them, will be constantly frustrated and upset.

  - ⊙ Trying to avoid or stop change is futile.

- You have to learn how and become skilled at adapting and adjusting in life. There is always a way, you just have to find it, and then change won't be so hard!

- You will embrace change when you are good at adapting and adjusting. It becomes enjoyable, just like anything else you are good at. You have to practice and play!

- You can adjust your body, mind, and intellect to adapt to any situation. You have that power. So, utilize that!

- When anything changes, think about what ways you can adapt and adjust. This way, you become resourceful and fearless of the ever-fluctuating world you live in!

- If you don't adapt and adjust you will suffer within yourself, your relationships, your career, and in the world as the world keeps turning.

- When you get good at adapting and adjusting yourself, you are like a chameleon in your ability to blend into your surroundings.

Power-Quote: "It is not the strongest of species that survives, nor the most intelligent that survives. It is the one that is most adaptable to change."

~Charles Darwin

The Family Emails

Adapting to the drastic changes in my life taught me how to effectively communicate with my family. My family loved us dearly and desperately wanted to help and support David and me. Having David's large family and friend circle coming and going so often, I had very little energy left. The small amount of time that nobody was around, was the only time for self-care. As much as my family wanted to physically show up, I needed them to stand down. A Jewish family does not back away from hardship easily. My family's intentions were pure and good, but I was unable to be responsive to them.

I felt burdened to answer questions as to how David and I were doing. The answers were too complex and draining to describe. Each text or phone call felt like a lead plate dropping on my head. One more thing to respond to when my cup was overflowing. Wishing to fall into the arms of my family for them to be around, and with David, there wasn't room for me to breathe. I had to find a way to communicate and let my family know what was going on, how I was, and how to best give their support. So, I began sending family emails. These emails were for my parents, siblings, and significant others. Family emails allowed me to vent without being on the phone or talking and using my voice. It gave me more control over checking my email and their replies than having my phone flooded with messages. I typed to update, keep them in the loop and reiterate what I needed; to laugh, smile, and be uplifted. I asked them NOT to send anything heavy and emotional to exacerbate deep sorrow and sadness. The process was very healing. I highly suggest this form of communication to be supportive of someone dying or having difficulty in life. Here are two of the family emails. One is from when David was still alive, and the other is after he passed.

Hello family,

It has been a while since the last check-in. David has turned a corner. We made it through a very intense time. The Duke Cancer team figured out why David was having seizures daily. The steroids were masking his new seizure threshold (after the second surgery, a new grade of cancer, a fresh hole in his head, the brain fry from radiation for six weeks). Each time he tried to taper down steroids the seizure symptoms would become worse and worse. So, after increasing his seizure dosage and adding in another drug he finally has relief from seizure symptoms and is stable. Now we have new symptoms from a triple dose of chemo and other treatments BUT those are not scary just annoying to him. We have a way to go to fully get off the steroids. He will be miserable for a couple of months because of this but hopefully won't seize out. The main symptoms of withdrawal are chronic fatigue (chemo makes him tired as well) and mood swings etc...

Funny story-time: David forgot to close our front gate on garbage day. I let the dogs out thinking the gate was closed. A few moments later I hear blood-curdling screams. I ran outside to see the dogs in the middle of the street and a lady across the street screaming bloody murder. The dogs came to me right away. She scared them off. I tried to say sorry numerous times and the gate was open etc... She screamed and screamed and then said while screaming "I had to throw my dog in the garbage can". She tipped it over and took her Pomeranian out of the can! She continued to SCREAM and call me names, so I joined in and called her names back (very adult of me, right?!). Yup, after she screamed at the top of her lungs for at least three full minutes and I apologized, I snapped. Anyways, that's my fun-filled story of the week!

On the plus side, you know David, he just cannot stop action unless he's dead. So, our house is coming along. By the end of this month, we should have our entire exterior done, the gate, fence, gutters, garage, and front landscaping!

Love you all and hope that you are holding up and staying healthy. Thank you for all your love and support from afar:)

C

Hey fam,

It's been a month since my beloved passed away and my heart is broken. This time of year, was David's favorite. Although I am feeling lighter and more energetic from the intensity and heaviness of caring for and watching him die, I am still grieving and probably will be for quite some time.

Each holiday David would get so excited. To be honest, I was not thrilled about going to his dad's or mom's and would let it be known. But I would begrudgingly go and of course, always have a great time. Last year we missed the holidays for our big trip and when we came home to our new house under construction and the unknown

Caren Paskel

second deadly tumor brewing, I lost it and left on Christmas day. This brings tears to my eyes as I write... He thought I was leaving him. It was painful but after coming home the next day and both of us expressing our deepest feelings we talked it through, and he understood that I was taking care of myself before totally snapping and would never leave him.

This holiday season I am choosing to honor my husband David as it brings much comfort, joy, and healing. I'm spending today at David's moms, where there will be many people. The crazy thing is that I am so looking forward to going! David would be so happy. Friends and other family members are coming by throughout the week and a couple of teachers and students to take my virtual yoga class on Sunday and Thanksgiving Day.

I would love and want to attend Thanksgiving with you, and my family, but due to my exposure to so many people, it's not a good idea. I love you and wish we could all be together. I hope you understand that my husband just died, and I need to do what's best for me. I am sorry if this disappoints any one of you.

I am happy to talk with you. However, threats won't help me grieve and move forward. Talking about my choices to others won't help me get through this holiday season without the love of my life. Lecturing isn't effective and will cause more stress. This is my way through the darkness of losing him. If that means some family members or friends don't want to be around me, I will have to deal with that on my own.

Hopefully, next year will be different. Love you all and thank you.

Love,

Care

The Power of Self-Belief

Power-Thought: Use Effective Communication

- ☀ Effective communication works. Ineffective communication doesn't work.

- ☀ How to effectively communicate:

  - ⊙ Who are you talking to? What kind of relationships do you have… Assess their personality/nature to know who you are communicating with.

  - ⊙ Where are you talking? The setting and environment will give you a lot of information as to how to communicate appropriately and effectively.

  - ⊙ When are you talking? What time of day are you talking? What's going on in their life and yours whatever the topic may be? What time of year is it and what's going on in the world?

  - ⊙ Has there been a big change or shift in you, them, or the world, since your last communication? How much time has passed…?

- ☀ Being honest is key to effectively communicating! When you are afraid of what others may say or think, you tend to hold back on communicating true thoughts and feelings.

- ☀ When it comes time to communicate in addressing an issue or just share, ask yourself if you are using effective communication:

  - ⊙ Who are you showing up as?

  - ⊙ Are you showing up as your highest best self?

  - ⊙ Or, are you showing up as a version of yourself from the past?

  - ⊙ What is your mindset?

  - ⊙ How are you holding space and carrying yourself?

- ☀ How would anyone else know what is going on or how to communicate with you if you don't let them know what's going on? What you may think is communicating, or making perfect sense, may not be clear to another.

- ☀ Finally, and this is a game-changer for all of your communication and relationships: TRY AND WORK TO UNDERSTAND AND THEN TO BE UNDERSTOOD.

  - ☉ It's in your understanding that you may be more understood.

  - ☉ Even if you are not understood, at least you understand why!

  - ☉ When you work to understand someone else you are thinking less about yourself. It's so much easier! When you come from a place of understanding, you may use effective communication to be understood!

Power-Quote: "To effectively communicate, we must realize that we are all different in the way we perceive the world and use this understanding as a guide to our communication with others."

- Tony Robbins

The Friends

In learning how to effectively communicate at the most stressful time of my life thus far, I also learned how to embrace and understand David's friends and their importance. As with our family, the number of friends I had were drastically outnumbered by David's. Being more introverted, I preferred to be alone most of the time while David was more extroverted, preferring to be around people most of the time. Thankfully, my few friends each played valuable roles in my life and were there for me when David was sick. My two besties from childhood and high school, Mer and Kell, knew me more than most and would do anything for me. They both dropped off items and groceries at the house. I could call them anytime and they would be there to cheer me up or just let me cry. Over the years, David and I went on infrequent double dates with both my besties and their hubbies. Each date was a

The Power of Self-Belief

memorable story! There was no dull date or moment with David no matter who we were with. His self-belief entertained and always brought everyone together to have a good time.

My adult bestie, Julie, became much more than a yoga student. We became closer to one another over the years and developed an incredibly dynamic friendship. Her kids were grown and she had the extra time to help in opening my yoga studio. Without the means to compensate a manager, her assistance was invaluable. She is a trusted friend and confidant whom I regularly communicate with, to this day. I call her my Julie. She truly was and is still my right-hand woman for my business and life. David always said, "I want a Julie". When David was sick, she held a strong and compassionate space and listened to me empathically. She knew how to reach out and when. She was a boulder that kept me grounded when I was unhinged. She stepped in to manage what I couldn't with no questions asked and zero expectations from me. Our deep understanding of one another molded a beautiful friendship, a relationship that we share and treasure.

Nan is my wild hippy child spiritual friend and a prior yoga student as well. Unlike me, she was unafraid to fully be seen. Her contagious vibrant energy brought me out of my shell. She's my soul-mother. Nan met her husband David before I met my husband, David. Her David had a giant presence as well and the two of them together were invigorating to be around! David and I had our first official date with Nan and her David at what became our regular date spot, *Bistro Joe's*. They became significant, not only because we shared our first date but because Nan's David, was diagnosed with cancer before my David's diagnosis. They were also battling cancer. Not a great commonality, but it brought us closer. David was able to talk to David and I could talk to Nan and we were able to relate to the struggles and find joy and laughter throughout the crazy cancer ride. They were at the hospital for both of David's surgeries. During hospice, Nan's David, being a robust man, was able to lift and move my David. The two David's hugged and exchanged heart-to-heart. I don't know what was said but I do know that Nan's David spoke loving and reassuring words to him. My David heard every one of them. The four of us were at such different stages and ages of our lives. Our Spiritual bond was mighty and unbreakable.

Last but certainly not least, only one of my friends, Courtney and her husband Michael, attended David and my extravagant Italian wedding. David had never met them before as they lived in Hawaii. We celebrated together as if we were all longtime friends. Courtney offered to photograph our beautiful event. She and I were roommates when we both lived in California. Initially, I was opposed to a tall, beautiful blond moving in with me and my boyfriend. As it turned out, she was my lifesaver, and we became best friends. While my relationship was in turmoil, her friendship lit up my life. Although we live so far away from one another, we keep in touch to this day.

Power-Thought: Wisely Choose Your Friends

- Be friendly with everyone but don't be friends with everyone! There's a huge distinction between who you are friendly and friends with; you may be friendly to many but who your friends are shows who you are.

- You get to decide whom you want to have as your friend as long as they decide they want you as their friend too.

- Take the time to think about who are the right friends to keep.

  - What qualities do they have and do those qualities add to your life?

  - How do they treat you?

  - Do they influence you positively or negatively?

- You are not in judgment; you are only ensuring you are in good company.

- Be selective in selecting your friends. You may have friends from the past who are unhealthy for you to be around. You may have many people who want to befriend you. Wisely choose those friends who add to your life and make you a better you.

- Know your areas of weakness and pick the right friends to fill in those gaps.

The Power of Self-Belief

- ☀ Look at your good friends, and ask yourself if they are a good model, mirror, and reflection of you. Would you want them to represent you?

- ☀ Your friends show a lot about who you are. Look closely at whom you call your friend.

> *Power-Quote: "Tell me who your friends are, and I'll tell you who you are."*

~Mexican Proverb

The Friend Circle

David's friend circle was an extension of his family. Each of his friends represented a part of David. All of his friends supported his growth in a particular way that allowed David to be who he was and maintain close friendships. When David was well and had friends over, I usually kept to myself. As he became sick, our circumstances changed. David's condition caused him difficulty working, communicating, and moving around. He was home most of the time except for doctor appointments. Our Cambridge home became the house of gathering. Initially, I felt bombarded. It took me way more time to become comfortable and warm up to David's family and friends. David had no problem getting along with anyone and everyone. The more people around, the more he felt at home. For me, it was the very opposite. The situation forced me, in a good way, to accept all who came into our home. I opened up to what was best for David and that in turn was best for me. His friends accepted me as well. We chose to be close and enjoy each other's company. We became one giant support system and a family. Each person played an imperative role. I could see and feel David was more at ease when his friends were surrounding him because he felt more like himself. The parts of him that were lost, his friends made up for. It's as though the missing pieces of himself rejoined. They were the glue that kept him feeling whole.

David had to completely downsize his growing business empire to only one partner. Stu started as David's intern around the same time David and I met. He grew close to David to become one of his dearest friends and most trusted business partners. Stu came over almost daily, as David could not take on the day-to-day workload. Stu and I clashed at first. Come to think of it, I clashed with all of David's friends! Stu was the rowdy loud friend that I rolled my eyes at and who always made fun of me. It was harmless, like annoying sibling banter. He loved David and was so good to him all the way through. He showed up each day thrilled to still be working with his buddy. Stu's loyalty to their partnership, friendship, and humor brought David joy and a sense of purpose. That melted my heart. Stu was very good to me too. He went above and beyond to help me through so much of the business that needed to be settled after David passed. I can't imagine how I would have done so without him.

Matt was David's best friend from high school. His story is quite interesting and somewhat unbelievable. They lived together before David and I did. They also had a working relationship. Matt came over regularly, even before David got sick, to be with his best friend. I was slightly bothered to come home from work and see his car parked on our driveway. I would say to him, "Matt why are you here?" And he would reply, "Hi Caren". But we were cool and more importantly, David was happy to have him over and spend time with him. When David got sick, Matt was at the Cambridge house a lot more. He was the third caregiver and conveniently lived nearby. He had also been through this before… When Matt was eighteen years old, his mother died from the same form of brain cancer David was diagnosed with. David was there for him at that time in his life. For Matt, going through the trauma of watching another loved one decline from glioblastoma brain cancer was unfathomable. Matt being there for me and David at the first hospital event was when I recognized how supportive David's friends were for both of us. They knew how much David loved me and so they loved me too. We all had to hold on to each other as David could not hold all of us up anymore. David needed to be supported and we did it together. It took a village. When Daniel wasn't home, Matt

The Power of Self-Belief

would be my go-to. It was comforting knowing that Matt had witnessed firsthand what David was going through. Mostly, he just wanted to be around David and help as much as he could. David was so weak and I was scared a lot of the time. I needed a ton of help and was calling Matt frequently to come by, especially when I thought David was about to seize or may need to be taken to the hospital.

Matt and Stu came over to both care for David and hang out. I became one of the boys, and we all had a great time together. This would have NEVER happened if David was well. They saved me. I would have sunk into an abyss if it were not for his friends. Two very close friends of David's, Carl and Mike, came by quite often as well. And those who lived a bit further, dropped by periodically. Jasmina, a long-term coworker and dear friend of David's brought over plenty of delicious baked goods from her family's bakery. One of David's friends from growing up was going through health struggles. He, too, was battling cancer sub-thirty. He was very sick and in the hospital for months at a time. David wanted to be there for him more than he was able to. David was so concerned for his well-being. They found solace in going through something very similar. He survived and David did not. Another one of David's dear friends was diagnosed with a very rare illness. Her husband and I unfortunately could understand and relate to what the other was going through. He and his beautiful wife got married despite her aggressive illness. We were invited to their very intimate wedding during COVID. Although I wanted to attend their wedding with David, it was more important for me to rest and take care of myself. Matt was close friends with them and was elated to take David and share quality time. It turned out to be the best decision for all of us. It was a challenge for David to make that wedding. But he and Matt showed up together and had a blast. I stopped feeling guilty about not being the one to be with David for everything because I knew that it gave his friends and family a chance to be with him too. The friends were all a godsend and a blessing.

Caren Paskel

Power-Thought: Build Your Army of Support

- ☀ The more support you have in your life the more supported you will be.

- ☀ There are many kinds and types of support systems that you may assemble including: friends, family, support groups, therapists, guides, teachers, mentors, coaches, gurus, doctors, health practitioners, schools, institutions, education, classes, social media private or public groups, online support, programs, courses, nature, activities, hobbies, documentaries, information, knowledge, textbooks, pets…

- ☀ Have an army of support for your protection. Build your army of support to lean in or fall back on them at all times.

- ☀ When you feel supported, it allows you to be more fearless in facing your greater challenges in life. You'll have the encouragement, backup, and assistance needed to get through.

- ☀ When you build your army of support you won't feel as if it's all on you or that you are all alone.

- ☀ Build a support system and team that's in place for you to triumph.

> *Power-Quote: "You can't achieve anything entirely by yourself. There's a support system that is a basic requirement of human existence. To be happy and successful on earth, you just have to have the people that you rely on."*

> ~Michael Schur

The Food

FOOD also provided a lot of support for us in going through an extremely trying time. David and I were both foodies and loved eating really good quality delicious food. We regularly enjoyed wonderful and exquisite dining experiences. We ate at the top restaurants with the top chefs in the world. David believed that he was worthy of the best

The Power of Self-Belief

experiences in life. Somehow, he managed to make nearly impossible reservations on short notice with sincere confidence.

The Prentice's are well known for food and the restaurant industry. David's uncle Matt, who passed away from cancer shortly after David, owned some of the best-rated restaurants in Detroit over his career. While Uncle Matt was very sick, he was still working, which was a common Prentice trait. He opened a new restaurant called *Three Cats*. After David's first surgery, Uncle Matt would come by our Parkside home and cook for us. We would invite some of David's family and friends over to eat the massive amounts of food he made and bond over home-cooked incredible meals. Food brought us together at a time of sadness and fear of the unknown. Eating together surrounded us with an abundance of love, laughter, and delight.

After David's second surgery, our hands were very full and we needed even more assistance. One of my dear sweet cousins, Rachel, reached out to me and asked if she could put a meal service together that family members and friends could be a part of if they wished to, in ordering and delivering food to us. Initially, David was opposed to the idea. He was trying his hardest to follow a very restrictive diet. I assured him of choosing what restaurants and foods we wanted and that this would help Daniel and me immensely. The meal service began and it was amazing. I had no idea how supportive this was going to be for all three of us. The pandemic and David being sick made going to the market and out to eat nearly impossible. Food that I did not have to make or cook was comforting and relieving. There was nothing more exciting to see than my beautiful cousins and family members pulling up to my home to drop off yummy food from our favorite places to eat including Uncle Matt's. We got to support our favorite restaurants during the Pandemic! David started to enjoy this special delivery treat. It was a special treat and gave us something to look forward to EATING GOOD FOOD together.

David's Aunt, another Prentice, also came by with massive amounts of scrumptious home-cooked food for us. If it were not for David being sick, I would not have gotten to know so many of David's family members. I'd much rather have David be here alive and well, but he's not. The new relationships and experiences that grew from David's cancer were a blessing. Food became a form of love and union.

Power-Thought: Quality of Life Over Quantity

- Quality of life is something that EVERYONE may want to consider at any age and stage of their life. Why wait for quality of life? You don't know when you are exiting, even if you are told otherwise, that may or may not be the case. What you do know is that you are here for a limited amount of time.

- Treating each day as if it were the last does not mean being impulsive.

- Rather than doing more to feel more accomplished, be present. When the mind worries over the past and has anxiety for the future it takes you right out of the present moment. Is that quality of life?

  - You may learn from your past and remember it for various reasons, or you can choose not to. You may think about and plan for your future.

  - When you live in the past or ahead in the future, your life passes by you.

- Having the right attitude makes a thought or action of higher quality. If you are having higher quality thoughts and actions your life will be of higher quality.

- Think about how you can create a quality life in every moment, through all of your experiences.

- Don't wait for your quality of life, as you don't know if you have tomorrow but you do know you have today.

> *Power-Quote: "The power of self-belief ensures the quality of your life because you believe you are worthy of nothing less."*

> **~Caren Paskel**

PHASE SEVEN

Divine Orchestration Plus Final Countdown

The Divine Goodbye

David and I made the most out of every moment we had together. September was the month of our wedding anniversary and our last outing. Brain cancer didn't stop David from living his life or commemorating it. Even when he felt awful and his body was malfunctioning, he pushed to make it through. Without self-belief, he would have been beaten down by what cancer took from him. He believed he was worthy of his health and living life joyfully. He believed he would beat terminal brain cancer and that every second he had, was an opportunity to do so. He showed me that self-belief gives you the power to live life on your own terms rather than what life throws at you. It was eye-opening. If he could do it, why couldn't I and everyone else?

Miraculously, we made it to *Bistro Joe's* for our third and final wedding anniversary. When we sat down, David began speaking the most heartfelt and impactful words ever spoken in our six years together. His eyes welled up and full-fledged tears began rolling down his face. David may have shed a tear here and there, but nothing to this extent. I sat in silence as he recited his goodbye to me. I was not ready to say goodbye but he was and he did. He finally saw in me that his mission was accomplished. He recognized my self-belief. He spoke an incredible acknowledgment and description of the person I had become over the time he knew me. Here's a synopsis of David's divine goodbye to me:

Caren, I always knew you had so much potential and would be successful in anything you decided to do. I did not see you becoming the fearless and successful woman you are today. You are a powerhouse. You are doing what I did not think you were fully capable of. You are killing it. You are taking care of me and you are taking care of business. Nothing and no one can stop you. Watching you brings me such joy. I am so proud of you, prouder than ever before. My wife is a badass and I could not be happier watching you thrive. My work is done here. I've got to inspire and teach you everything I know and you are doing it! I am ok and happy to die because I know you are going to be ok and don't need me anymore...

He was speaking to and through me as my angel on earth to ignite my self-belief. His work was completed and he was ready to move on to the next chapter of his journey. Listening and soaking his words into my every cell, transferred his self-belief onto me. We saw right through one another. It was truly a magical moment. There was no more resistance, not an ounce, and no more struggle. David was mentally at peace. He had accepted his fate. Yes, he still wanted to live, but he surrendered to the chance he may not. Nothing more needed to be spoken about that evening. We shared an unforgettable last anniversary.

Power-Thought: Reach for Your Greatest Potential

- ☀ A human being is born into the world to gain or reach their full potential, the pinnacle of their perfection. The biggest clue is that you were born as a human being. Humans are the only species that can choose to develop and improve themselves and their life.

  - ⊙ You can choose to work on your physical health to be in better shape.

  - ⊙ You can choose to work on your emotional and intellectual state for mental health.

  - ⊙ You can choose to focus on the material or the spiritual. You can improve or worsen yourself. You can believe in yourself or not.

  - ⊙ The choice is yours!

- ☀ Nobody can reach your great potential for you; you have to do it yourself. This is not to say you don't need a lot of help and support. However, your self-effort is independent and can only be done by you. You can choose to take a different path, change your career, etc.... NO OTHER SPECIES HAS THESE CHOICES!

- ☀ You have nothing to lose by reaching for your ultimate greatness within yourself. Think about what a slightly better version of yourself might look and feel like. How would that affect your happiness, confidence, relationships, career, and impact on the world?

- ☀ If through self-development you don't become more peaceful and happier, and if your life does not become better and better then you can end the pursuit and pursue whatever you want!

- ☀ Reaching your greatest potential is your purpose. Your life becomes extraordinary and one that the world benefits from. It's a win-win!

- ☀ You must believe in yourself to reach for your greatest potential.

> *"The purpose of life is to discover your gift. The work of life is to develop it. The meaning of life is to give your gift away."*

~David Viscott

The Last MRI

David had a gift. He used his life to develop his gift and gifted me and countless others. His condition was worsening and he could barely walk. The next MRI at Duke was his last. The waiting period was highly stressful so we did what we did best, we wined and dined at the hotel in NC. One glass of wine for me is my usual but that night I had two. I have been told that two drinks Caren is a blast! When we got up to the room, instead of dreading the next day or mentally agonizing. I danced around the room to some music. David sat on the couch with a big grin and watched. We laughed together and spent a very special memorable night in each other's arms. Rather than worrying about future results, we highlighted our love.

The next day, we held hands and showed up for the unavoidable news. It's hard to describe the feeling of waiting for results. We were going to face whatever we had to. Nothing was over until it was over. When the team arrived with MRI results, the images were almost unbelievable. Cancer spread all over his entire brain. We were all in shock to see the drastic and dramatic change that occurred in only two months. Dr. Friedman and nurse Rosemary stayed positive and told us that they were going to treat this more aggressively and try a new form of chemo. David was up for anything. I was devastated. My heart sunk and my stomach knotted up. It was hard to breathe. It took everything in me not to externally express my internal meltdown. I went out into the waiting area and burst into sorrowful tears. Rosemary came to check on me as she knew I was going to lose it. She looked me straight in the eye with the confidence I needed and said, "Caren you are going to be ok. We are going to try this treatment and it may work. Let's stay positive". That was the slap of belief I needed to snap out of my deep sadness and fear of losing my husband. I pulled it together and did not break down further in front of David. Later on, I found out how in shock the Duke team was as to David's MRI. Nurse Rosemary confided in me that Dr. Friedman had never seen brain cancer spread so rapidly in such a short amount of time. I did not share this with David but I knew that David's time here on earth was running out.

Delivering the awful news to his mom and dad was despairing but I did my best to keep them hopeful. They were crushed, of course. That night was not so cheerful, it was just too hard for both of us. On the flight home, our hands were held tightly together. Unending tears rolled down my face. I knew I was going to lose him.

The Power of Self-Belief

Power-Thought: Show Up Rather Than Give Up

- ☀ You have a choice when life gets tough. You can toughen up and show up fully or you can shut down, throw in the towel and give up. When you give up, you are only giving up on yourself. You are failing YOU! When you believe in yourself you show up even when you want to give up.

- ☀ Shutting down may seem like the easy way out. Shutting down only shuts you down and others out from helping you.

- ☀ Showing up opens up for answers, solutions, support, and ways through.

- ☀ When you want to give up, run away, quit, hide or end it all, think about what that is going to do for you and those surrounding you. Showing up uplifts while giving up pulls you and others down. Stop being selfish and show up for yourself.

- ☀ Showing up for yourself empowers you and others around you.

> *Power-Quote: "Courage starts with showing up and letting ourselves be seen."*
>
> **~Brene Brown**

The Move Downstairs

Although the MRI results were horrendous, David and I were not going to give up when we got home from North Carolina. The new chemo and advancement of cancer took a huge toll on David. He slept most days. Daniel took the nighttime caregiving shift and I took the daytime one. It worked out for a very short period. We tried everything we could to care for him on our own. We moved a bed downstairs on the main floor for David's safety. He could barely stand up or walk. It was becoming too difficult for us to lift or move him. Friends and family were unequipped as well. We could no longer properly care for him on our own. The reality of David's condition was heart-wrenching.

David's sister Jackie was a nurse's assistant. She stayed nights with him at the hospital post-surgery and offered to stay the night at our home when David moved downstairs. She was used to the night shifts and slept on our couch next to her big brother. One morning she was very distraught at how bad David's condition had progressed. David's father convinced Daniel and me to take David to the hospital. The hospital recommended calling EMS for assistance in escorting him to the hospital. He could not walk on his own at this point. Thank goodness they were kind enough to transfer David into my car via gurney and prop him up in the passenger seat. David's body was giving out. He reached for my phone charger as if it were a urine container and started urinating all over the seat and himself. It was a messy drive, but we made it to the hospital safe and sound… That was a miracle in itself. There was no time to doubt or fear. The power of self-belief took over to act fast without hesitation.

David despised being admitted to the hospital. We had no choice. Daniel and I both knew what this meant, the new treatment wasn't working. One thing was for sure, my strong courageous husband was NOT going to die in the hospital, hell no! My mission was for David to pass away in the comfort of our own home, where he was committed to renovating and making it beautiful for us, surrounded by the love of our closest family, friends, and baby boy Onyx. My self-belief remained intact. Everyone was emotional and distraught. Each family member had their opinion as to what they thought was best for David. Knowing what David wanted, I didn't allow the clamor of emotions to upset or disturb my ability to discern and decide how to proceed. I had a plan and was intent on making it happen. The power of my self-belief led me through each step. Proper hospital equipment and professional help were organized and set in place for his homecoming. He would spend his last days in our home and not in the hospital. Mission accomplished.

Power-Thought: Trust Your Judgment

- You don't have to trust or judge anyone else. The only person you can truly trust is yourself.
- Use intellect to judge and decide what is right and best for you.
- When you learn to trust your judgment, you can hear it! Listen to and follow your inner voice of reason.
- Become clear of your deeper knowing that nobody else knows but you. Trust that inner knowing to be your life guide.
- When you worry over what others are saying or doing, you are being selfish! Yes, you are worried about YOU rather than doing what's best.
- In trusting your judgment, you do what's right rather than allowing external voices, personalities, or differences of opinions to overpower your decisions and actions. They will

become whispers in your background. Your trust is in the foreground and leads you.

☀ Trust your judgment to plow ahead and nothing will knock you down.

> *Power-Quote: "Believe nothing, no matter where you read it or who has said it, not even if I have said it unless it agrees with your own reason and your own common sense."*

~Buddha

The Caregiver and Hospice Angels

In trusting my judgment, I was able to get the professional aid that we needed immediately. David's cancer was spreading and could not be stopped. He was going to die sooner than later. In coming to terms with my husband's death, I decided to have full time in-home care as well as hospice until his end. We needed a ton of support and help to get through this and I wanted David to be as comfortable and cared for as possible.

I hired a highly recommended and rated caregiving company that was able to start right away. Every conversation with the main nurse was loving and kind. Her voice alone calmed me. What a godsend she was. This beautiful being worked to ensure that every caregiver on rotation was doing their job effectively, Daniel and I were pleased, and David was in the best hands. Daniel and I were alleviated. We could spend more quality time with David. It was relieving and nurturing to have family, friends, and rotating caregivers in our home at all times. We all came together for David.

The caregivers were there around the clock and could also keep track of and administer David's medications and drugs if and when needed. They helped with his food and eating, kept him clean, changed him, and rotated his body to avoid bed sores. There were a few caregivers that not only cared for David but for Daniel and me as well. They essentially took twelve-hour shifts and were living with us. We got

The Power of Self-Belief

to know them and they were all little angels who floated in and out serving with smiles and love. Everyone was working as a team and David was not in pain. He could not speak or walk. He ate and slept most of the time. He nodded and communicated through hand signals. He heard everything but was slowly fading away.

My father had given me a number to call for a hospice service at the time of hiring the caregivers. The woman I conversed with over the phone was incredibly kind and soothing. She told me a hospice nurse would be reaching out to explain and guide me on what to do next and the process. When the nurse called, I picked up the phone and she spoke, "Hello Caren, do you remember me? I used to be one of your regular yoga students…" My heart exploded knowing she was one of my most cheerful yoga students back in the day who was always smiling! She brought energy to every class that uplifted me and everyone around her. Heather was my past yoga student and my present hospice nurse. Upon her arrival, I buried myself in her arms. I was elated to let the family know of our connection and that David was in the very best care and hands. She was outstanding. What an angel. We were so blessed. We had earth angels shining their light on us in a time of heavy despair.

Power-Thought: Attracting Earth Angels

- ☀ When you think of angels you may think of after-life or some unknown universal force coming from the heavens above. Look around rather than up in the sky for the angels that emerge in your life, or someone else's right here on earth. They are alive. You may be one!

- ☀ Earth angels are people and animals who shine their light and leave a mark in your life. They offer guidance or unexpectedly support you. Earth angels gift you with who they are and their presence feels angelic. They most likely come and go like a breeze, or perhaps they stay for a while.

- ☀ There is no need to ask or pray for earth angels. It's your power of self-belief that attracts them.

Caren Paskel

☀ Believe you are worthy of receiving the blessings of earth angels and they shall come.

> *Power-Quote: "Some people appear in your life when you need them most. They love you and lift you, reminding you of the best, even when you're going through the worst. These people are not just friends, they are earth angels."*

> **~Ann Taylor**

The Last Ten Days

For ten days our home was filled with earth angels, friends, and family members visiting and saying their goodbyes. David remained the life of the party even on his deathbed. While awake, David was the center of our company. If he was getting changed or washed, as soon as that was over, I would ask, "David, honey do you want your friends to come in here?" Every time he would nod his head, yes. He found comfort in his dear ones gathering around. He smiled and even laughed when his friends were sitting on the couch on each side of his bed. It was not easy for any of us to see David so still and quiet. We were aware he would not be here for long and wanted to bring him as much joy as possible. That's what he thrived on even in his last ten days. Each night I'd wedge my body beside him in the narrow hospital bed. I felt and heard his heartbeat on the side of my face thumping away as he held me tight with his left hand and arm. He was very much alive, and I did not want to let go.

David went through his last days as a true champion and warrior. Cancer had not taken away his spirit. Family and friends celebrated around him for ten days straight. We ate amazing meals that were brought and cooked for us. One night his stepsisters, came by. It was just what I needed, a girls' night! They brought so much laughter to the house, and I joined them in drinking some champagne. We brought our energy around David, and I snuggled up next to him. He put his hand on my butt and squeezed as we all giggled. David was never shy about showing me affection. I held on to every moment, holding myself together for him to see me as his loving, happy wife.

One of my gurus passed down the following message to me when my husband was terminally diagnosed. His words helped me recognize the right attitude to keep: *When you visit a friend lying in the hospital you must consider yourself lucky. Think you could be lying there. The message is that you and I are standing and commenting on a person lying in bed. Remember you and I could be lying there and he was standing looking at us. You and I can pass off before him. You have taken it for granted that you will live and that he will die. As soon as a human is born, he is susceptible to death. If you expect it, you are a pessimist. The problem is that you are unprepared for death when it is inevitable. Therefore, you must do your best and get on with life.*

Caren Paskel

Power-Thought: Honor Your Journey

- ☀ If your focus is on death, you lose your life. If you focus on someone else's death, you forgot you may die too. It's easy to get caught up in someone else's journey.

- ☀ Focus on your journey and never take one second for granted even when another's life is hanging by a thread.

- ☀ Each person has their own journey. You have yours and they have theirs. Getting entangled in someone else's journey is disrespectful of yours and disruptive to theirs. Respect the laws of nature.

- ☀ Honor your journey and that each being has its own. Various people may enter and exit along the way. While you play your role in life, understand that each is on their own journey, including YOU!

> *Power-Quote: "Note that this journey is uniquely yours, no one else's path has to be your own. You cannot imitate somebody else's journey and still be true to yourself. Are you prepared to honor your uniqueness in this way?"*

-Jon Kabat - Zinn

The Last Supper

When David was in hospice, his diet was no longer a concern. Amazingly, he was able to eat until the day before he died. His appetite was more than healthy, most likely due to steroids. He enjoyed the hell out of eating. I fed him whatever he wanted whenever he wanted. Why take that away from him when there was nothing left? I was grateful we took pleasure in eating together up until his very end. For the duration of hospice, the food kept coming and with more surprises.

Before David became very ill, he opened his own real estate company, "Home Team Detroit". His office was located in New Center, Detroit. After David's seizure, by law, he was not permitted to

The Power of Self-Belief

drive for six months I became his driver. Driving David to work we passed a restaurant named *Cuisine,* which closely resembled the quaint homes along the same street. We were curious. David finally dined at *Cuisine* with one of his Irish business partners. He messaged me during their dinner raving about the experience, "*Cuisine* is the best restaurant in Detroit and I cannot wait to take you". The exceptional French cuisine was indeed divine. Chef Paul came out to introduce himself and that was the beginning of our relationship and also our new hot date spot. We couldn't get enough and we indulged! We gave Chef Paul full reign in designing and creating our meals without looking at the menu or price! We would go all out when we were there. We felt like we were on vacation, in Detroit. The chef surprised us with new concoctions paired with the perfect wine. We were happy to expose our new find to our family and friends' foodies. Countless wonderful memories were shared at *Cuisine* with each other and loved ones.

Chef Paul reached out to me during David's last days and asked if he could hand-deliver a meal for all of us. I started crying knowing how much this would mean to David. David was always one to surprise me and now it was my time to surprise him! Chef Paul and his lovely assistant, whom David and I adored, came over to our home with glorious platters of our favorite French dishes. David smiled, laughed, and gave a huge thumbs up for this meal and visit. It was outstanding. A perfectly filling royal last supper for David to relish.

Power-Thought: Live to Be Giving

- ☀ True giving is carrying an attitude of service and sacrifice without wanting anything in return. Giving has nothing to do with getting. Giving is opposed to taking.

- ☀ Result-oriented actions spoil your giving. You will be mentally disturbed thinking about the result.

- ☀ When you live to give you will be at peace. When you live to take you will be stressed and suffer. It's that simple. Try it out and feel the difference.

  - ☉ Live to be giving - expectations = happiness

- ⊙ Live to be getting + expectations = unhappiness

- ⚜ Giving does not have to be big gestures or to do with anything monetary. Adjust your attitude to what can I do for you? If there's someone in the grocery store line with a few items while your cart is full, wave them ahead, "you first".

- ⚜ As you live to be giving, you won't be concerned for yourself, and what you are going to get. Without being worried about yourself you feel happier, lighter, and freer.

- ⚜ If giving does not bring you the most amount of joy in your living, you are not truly giving.

- ⚜ When you are truly giving you are fully living!

Power-Thought: "Only by giving are you able to receive more than you already have."

-Jim Rohn

The Last Prayer

Living to give created divine experiences leading up to David's death. On day nine of hospice, David's sweet mother Michelle sensed her son's near end of life. There was an urgency in her voice when she called. She thought David and I would have an affinity toward a young priest, Father Mark, to give David his last prayer, blessing, and funeral sermon when the time came. She wanted him to come to the house. It meant a lot to her. More love, kindness, and prayer could not hurt. A kind man arrived at our home. Daniel and I huddled together around David. Father Mark praised and sang his prayers. I did not care if a priest or a rabbi was there. It was healing for Daniel and me. We believed in David's life, soul and spirit. We needed all the forms of belief to aid us through his passing. Recognition of something greater brought us peace in watching David fade. We had a divine encounter without judgment or skepticism.

Michelle and I became a united team. We spoke daily. She had a feeling David was going to die the next day and she was right. She said, "Caren I have a feeling I need to be there tomorrow. It is the birth date of my mother". Even though the hospice nurse presumed David would live many more days, possibly a month, a mother knows her son. Her intuition that the time was coming sooner than later, the next day, was correct. David's mom and I formed an unbreakable spiritual bond. We believed in David and the love we had for him brought us together.

Power-Thought: Self-Belief Is Reunion

- Self-belief is a belief that there is something greater within to reunite. Eminence resides in one and all.

- The majority of humanity spends most of their time searching and seeking outwardly to find happiness. You will come to find that anything material is ephemeral. The world is impermanent.

- If you are fed up with the chase for your happiness, look within. You have the most valuable treasure of all.

- Your power of self-belief is a reunion to your enduring happiness.

- Self-belief has and always will be who you essentially are. You have strayed so far that you are separated. Separation from your self-belief is what causes you to feel empty and pushes you toward people, places, and things. You will be temporarily filled up and satiated. The cycle is endless.

- When you turn inward, you fill up by reuniting with your self-belief. As you continue to merge with your power of self-belief, you get fuller. You will feel more relief and less pressure to run after things and beings. The inward pursuit will bring you more peace and happiness, the kind that lasts...

Power-Quote: "If you establish serenity and happiness inside yourself, you provide the world with a solid base of peace. If you do not give yourself peace, how can you share it with others? If you do not begin your peace work with yourself, where will you go to begin it?"

-Nhat Hanh

The Epic Seizure

David entered another stage, before death, of total peace without pain or suffering. And because of this, I was at peace. With the advancement of cancer, we were astonished he hadn't seized for nine days in hospice. David once disregarded sleep at all costs and wanted to conquer the world with his ever-growing vision. It was baffling to see him lying lifeless and slipping into eternal sleep. This was his journey. David was in solace nearing his end and ready to transition to the next chapter whatever that was. Like everything he did, from his marriage proposal to the day he died, it was a sensational event.

On day nine of hospice, David's sister Jackie came by to visit. I was driving home from an appointment with a health practitioner about forty-five minutes away. Every week I went to see her for nutritional support after my pancreatitis attack. The beautiful woman with long luxurious black hair and perfectly smooth glowing skin was soothing and healing to me during this hectic time. She listened to my story as it unfolded, in awe of how I was still standing. Another beautiful earth angel. This was part of my self-preservation in caring for David.

Thirty minutes from home, the dreaded phone call came from Daniel. He notified me that David was seizing. I called the hospice nurse immediately. She instructed the caregivers on how much morphine and Ativan to administer to David. Upon my arrival home, he was still seizing… it had been almost an hour. In the past, his seizures lasted no longer than a minute or so, which seemed like an eternity. This was something else. Watching him seize for so long was agonizing. I desperately wanted the nightmare to end. There was only one thing that got me through and held me up. The power of self-belief kept me strong, fully present, and wide awake for David.

Once the hospice nurse arrived, she took control of the situation. She loaded him with more drugs. From the neck down, David's body was healthy, his organs were strong, and still fighting brain cancer to stay alive. That's why his last seizure was epically long. She also told us that she had never given as much morphine to a person before. I stayed by his side the entire time and held his hand. He was still holding on and squeezing back. We were very much connected. He wasn't alone, I was right there. The power of self-belief held me up for him even though all I wanted to do was scream, cry and run away.

David's mother arrived toward the end of the seizure. At that point, it was us two, she on his right side and me on his left. It took two full hours of rotating between two narcotics to stabilize his body from seizing. The hospice nurse assured David was stable and had some time left, perhaps days. The epic seizure took everything out of both David and me. He was snoring and I was shaking from head to toe. I went upstairs and drew a bath to calm my nerves. David's mom frantically knocked on my bedroom door, "Caren, something isn't right, you need to come back down" I whipped my clothes back on and ran downstairs. David's skin had turned pale and he was struggling to breathe. In a very composed manner, I looked at David's mom and said, "Michelle I think he has passed". She said he had a pulse. I called up the hospice nurse and told her that David was passing away and she needed to turn around and come back to the house immediately. When she arrived, she said he was still there… but I knew he wasn't.

Power-Thought: Nature Has a Plan

- ☿ Allow nature to take its course. There are stages that all beings go through in life from birth to death however long that may be.

- ☿ When you resist Mother Nature and her divine timing you become a controller. Controllers try to control the uncontrollable which is impossible! Trying to control factors that are beyond your control will cause undue stress, anxiety, worry, and a tremendous amount of your time and energy. And for what?

- ☿ Mentally surrender to the natural laws at play.

- ☿ Because you depend on external people, places, and things, for your happiness you want to have control over them. What you don't realize is that your attachments are controlling you!

- ☿ The only thing you have control over is your own self! Work on that and leave the rest alone.

- ☿ There is a way to be detached without being closed off. You can feel it and still deal. With a greater understanding of life and how it works, you play your part and watch the beautiful procession. Everything comes and goes.

> *Power-Quote: "The more you try to control something, the more it controls you. Free yourself, and let things take their own natural course."*

~<u>kushandwizdom.tumblr.com</u>

The Last Breath

Nature had a plan. David's time to exit his physical form had come. His mother and I communicated through a deep understanding and interconnection. Less words were expressed. We were hyper-focused on honoring David's transition. She looked at me and said, "you should be with him alone". She walked away and there we were, David and I together bound in our love. The power of my self-belief completely

The Power of Self-Belief

took over. He transferred his self-belief onto me. I took his hand in mine, resting my head on his chest and listened to his exhausted heartbeat. In a firm and loving tone, I gave precise instructions, rather than permission to die. My final words to my beloved were, "Honey, it's time for you to go. I love you. You are ok. I am ok. You don't have to fight anymore. You are ready." His mother and I intuitively changed places. We locked eyes as we passed one another. She went to his side and I went upstairs to slide my body into a warm bubble bath. The glass of champagne I brought up minutes before was awaiting. David took his last breath the moment I stepped away from him. I messaged my family members to let them know, "David has passed away. Cheers to David The Champion." I took a sip and toasted to my husband's power of self-belief and the strongest, bravest man I had ever known to love in the flesh. I felt immense gratitude rather than loss.

After my bath, while I spent a few moments alone, the hospice nurse called me from downstairs. I was aware David was gone. I told her that I would be down shortly. As I exited my bedroom, one of David's best friends, Carl, was in the hallway. He came upstairs to tell me the news that I already knew. We embraced. Carl had tears streaming down his face. When I came down, David's mouth was open, no more breath, and his skin had turned to violet. I took one more look. I chose to keep the healthy vibrant image of who he was to be imprinted in my mind and not his spiritless body. I walked away, greeted and wept with the family and friends that came to say their goodbyes to David's vacant body.

Power-Thought: Death Is Rebirth

- Death of life is the rebirth of something else.

- Take the time to think about life. Reflect and extract the essential teachings of religion and philosophy. Do your investigation.

- Nothing is ever gone. Life is changing and recycling into many other forms.

- Birth and death are simply an exchange. We cannot see or know what's next or what exactly happens at all times.

- We do know the law of conservation of energy that states the amount of energy is neither created nor destroyed.
  - ⊙ Where does energy move upon death?
  - ⊙ Where does a newborn baby acquire its unique personality from?

- Inquire into life and think for yourself! Go as far as your thinking can carry you. Go to make some sense out of life. You may take up or dismiss anything you want.

- We are going through death and rebirth daily. A day begins and ends. Seasons begin and end. Infancy ends and childhood begins.... Childhood begins and ends. This goes perennially. You experience so many births and deaths daily and think nothing of it.

- Your experiences have birth and death. You began reading this phase of the book and now it is ending for a new phase to begin! The birth and death lifecycle goes on and on.

Power-Quote: "Birth and death are just passages, not of life but of time."

~Sadhguru

PHASE EIGHT

Celebrations Plus Life After Loss

The Million Dollar Death

David's passage occurred on October 20th, 2020. I was never a numbers person or into signs and symbols. However, I do believe in life and death and that each one of us has a journey. I believe that this existence is one of many chapters in our evolution until we reach the 100th mark, our greatest potential, and perfection. The date David died is undeniably symbolic: 10/20/2020. In terms of money, which was one of David's favorite things to make, that comes out to be $10,202,020! David always wanted to talk numbers with me. He valued himself and believed he was worthy. That's why money came so easy. Not because he was the smartest guy or the best at what he did. Nor was it about fame, power, or good looks. David had CBB, an acronym that my mentors instilled in me that stands for Confidence, Bravery, and Belief in yourself! David naturally had CBB, as if he was born with it.

After David passed, I decided to make the best use of his life insurance by investing in my self-development and carrying his legacy while creating mine. I am keeping him alive with *The Power of Self-Belief* as he graciously exemplified. I plan on earning $10,202,020 in the next few years.

You are worthy of millions if you choose to believe. You can decide to do a lot of good with your money. David's life was worth millions and each dollar I earn after his death is a symbol of his self-belief, making him proud and building a non-profit foundation in his honor; *DMP Spiritual Education Foundation*. I am doing this for him, me, and everyone who wants to have the power of their self-belief.

Caren Paskel

Power-Thought: Self-Belief Brings Abundance

- ☀ When you believe in yourself you tap into your inner wealth and abundance.

- ☀ The Universe is abundant. You are a part of the Universe. Therefore, you are abundant! When you believe you are abundant, that's what comes to you!

- ☀ Opposed to the abundant mindset is the scarcity mindset. A scarcity mindset repels your abundance.

- ☀ There are two extremes when it comes to material wealth.

  - ⊙ There are those who run after wealth with zero content. They may get into trouble doing so or break the law.

  - ⊙ There are those who push wealth away by abstaining. This will lead to suppression.

- ☀ There's a healthy way to contact and normalize wealth. Think of being wealthy as your natural birthright, but not in a materialistic way. The glorious divine spirit and soul, the unknown enlivening factor that runs through the Universe and all beings is abundance! You are wealthy already. Look at Mother Nature again. She is abundant, even with human interference.

- ☀ The right attitude toward material wealth is to always be happy with what you have and you may plan for more.

- ☀ Through the power of self-belief, you will be abundant!

> *Power-Quote: "Abundance is not something we acquire. It is something we tune into."*
>
> ~Wayne Dyer

The Celebration of Life

David was abundant inside and out. He wanted his life to be celebrated rather than mourned. He assuredly expressed that what he wanted was to be cremated and for everyone to have a party in his honor. Those were his two asks. He wished to be celebrated and remembered for the life he lived and the impact he made. I honored his wishes and stayed clear of family conflicts or drama. Accepting David's life and death journey allowed me contentment until his end and thereafter. He couldn't bear to think about his loved ones suffering from losing him. Agonizing over his death and our loss would be dishonorable. We were instructed to commemorate his life.

His parents agreed on having a proper funeral at a beautiful church nearby. I welcomed and remained open-hearted about every opportunity that was healing and brought togetherness. We were stronger together and needed one another like no other time. I embraced each of David's family members and friends. David's parents and I met at the church to speak with the priest and share our David stories. We had so much to say and wanted a chance to do so at his funeral. I wore a lovely, brightly floral-designed dress and spoke first to eulogize, celebrate, and emanate his power of self-belief. My memorial to my husband:

Our Two-Part True Love Story

Over the last six years, David and I had a two-part true love story. He was 24 and I was 36. We met online. I had let go of the idea of a soulmate and was not expecting anything to come of it. He was a young stud who was playing around with online dating. When we first met, I'll never forget the smile that emerged. It was as if he was looking at a goddess. He commented, "you're way more beautiful in person than in your pictures". And, that's how I felt when he looked at me - even up until his last moments, before the final day when his eyes never opened again.

For me, David's drive and mental determination attracted me more than his giant biceps and good looks (of course, that was a bonus!) I was refreshed by his logical thinking and outlook on life, his lofty goals, and the bizarre combination of being stubborn and also so loving and kind. He saw someone different from any other woman he had dated before. I had a career and was living very independently. I had a life, goals, and a plan too that he found both refreshing and attractive. He was on a mission and was ready to win at life and so was I. We were a perfect team! It truly was love at first smile and first sight. That was it and we never looked back. We became an unstoppable couple.

David and I were well aware of the age difference but it wasn't important to either of us. We defined our relationship and we did not ask for permission from family or friends. For our reasons, we weren't interested in the idea of marriage. We came from two very different backgrounds or sides of the tracks, but that did not matter either! In many ways, we were opposites. And that's what brought us together. We complemented each other. We were both, figuratively, on a rising ladder. We boosted each other up with each rung and continued climbing. David is still climbing.

There was no falling in love when it came to David and me. There was just rising and growing. And it was a natural progression. In less than a year of dating, we were sitting in the car after a yoga class. (Let the record show he did not like yoga! I never made him go but I am certain he came to look at my butt in yoga pants…) Anyway, he was speechless. His eyes were a bit watery, and he said, "I'm in love with you".

Shortly after that, we were lying side-by-side and he was speechless again. After a few moments of silence, he said, "I think I want to marry you". As soon as I said "me too", that was it! If you know David, you know that when he wants something he goes after it until he gets it! Shortly after, I received the proposal of a lifetime! He had it all set up, from the walk outside around the park at the most beautiful restaurant and hotel, that was our favorite spot, to a rose petal path leading to a huge heart on the bed and him on one knee with the ring I chose and never knew he bought. What a man! He did it right and it was perfect. The best night of my life. We were in no rush to get married but we both knew we wanted to be with nobody else. We sealed the deal with our engagement that lasted 2 years. We took our time because we had a lot to do! And we did it. We were both building and opening our businesses. Yes, simultaneously. He supported me tremendously and taught me so much. I was able to make my career dreams come true because of him. He showed, lived, and taught me that "Can't Doesn't Exist".

I did it and he did it and we were growing ourselves, our relationship, and our businesses. We wined and dined and traveled all over the world. David saw life as one big adventure. He wanted to live life fully and experience everything!

Our wedding and marriage are impossible to explain. I think we had three wedding parties or maybe even 4! Glenn, David's father, married us legally at our new beautiful home in Detroit on Parkside. We had a separate wedding brunch, dinner, and a wedding weekend bash at a lake-house where all our friends and family could join us in our celebration at their leisure.

But OUR plan was over the top. We went on a 2-week extravagant trip that began in Lake Como Italy. We went all out. David secured a yellow Ferrari. We sped off and arrived at this gorgeous hotel on the lake that looked like a castle. My parents flew in and one of my best friends and her husband came too. That was it! We had the perfect night on the water with a mountain across the lake. My father married us again, but this time David and I shared our special vows. We gorged on a meal that had so many courses I could not keep track. From there we drove our hot car to Switzerland. It was the most treacherous drive ever(!) and of course the most magnificent. But for David, as you know, everything had to be dangerous and thrilling. He loved challenging himself and challenging me, pushing limits and living on the edge. We went hang-gliding in the Swiss Alps, and then made our way to Zurich. Our final stop was Rome and what a way to end the trip. We rented a Vespa and nearly got killed numerous times. We saw the most beautiful art and ruins. The food and wine on this venture were out of this world and David was never prouder of me than when I ate an entire Italian pizza all by myself.

That's part one of our true love story - the fairy tale. Of course, there is one more special addition. I'm a dog person. David is not. But when one of my dogs passed, he surprised me with a puppy. Truly, I did not see this coming! My dogs agitated him so much. But, that's how much he loved me - that he was willing to live with my dogs and get another one! I know that was a sacrifice for me and my happiness. And of course, we didn't go for just any dog. We went for the small horse, our Great Dane Onyx. We traveled to Ohio to meet the breeder to pick up our beautiful boy. I was in heaven.

Two weeks after we brought Onyx home, David collapsed from a seizure, only one year after our wedding. This is where part two of our true love story began. Brain cancer changed everything. But not in the ways that most would think. Yes, I was

Caren Paskel

scared and sad and we both had to reevaluate everything. Our lives were flipped upside down but we did not flip out. We refocused. We focused on rule one that David outlined later in his book. "Focus on what matters".

Because of brain cancer, our relationship grew into something extraordinary. I had to step up in ways I never knew I could or would and I did. We were also blessed to have Daniel, one of David's younger brothers living with us. As a team, the three of us had to figure out how to move forward and work together. The last two years with two brain surgeries, tons of recovery, lots of medications, supplements, training, doctors, therapists, research, disabilities, seizures, hospitals, radiation, chemo, and traveling to Duke University all were David's choices that I fully supported. I learned to be a caregiver and he learned how to care for himself because he wanted to live as long as he could.

There was never an obstacle David did not overcome. He never once looked at brain cancer as a death sentence. By choice, he did not live like he was dying. In fact, despite all of this we still wined and dined. We traveled to Ireland and drove across the entire country. We went on our most epic trip since Italy, to Amsterdam, South Africa, and Paris… Our one-month adventure was cut short due to physical issues that we later found out to be a second deadly tumor. We came home to an impossible situation of a new house under construction, a second surgery and then a pandemic. But that did not stop David from living life, moving towards goals, and pushing himself beyond his limitations.

I will never know another man like David Prentice. Truly, there is no other like him. He was a gift I treasured for 6 years. He changed me forever. I am someone whom I thought I could never be or become. Part 2 of our true love story was a blessing for both of us even though that might sound crazy. We chose to see it as an opportunity. We grew as individuals and as husband and wife. We grew closer to our own families and one another's. What I have gained with David is way more than I have lost since his death. His love, friendship, and guidance will never be lost. I will carry that forever.

I shared with him fully becoming himself beyond succeeding in business. Brain cancer was a teacher to David - not an enemy. He became someone he thought he would never be or become. I got to watch and go through it with him.

Since he was no longer working 4 am-8 pm at the office, he was at home and got to see me become the best version of myself. He was blown away and marveled at that, which is hard to do if you know him. How do I know? He told me about it at our 3rd wedding anniversary, this September. With tears streaming down his face. I had never seen him cry like this before. He told me the truth. In essence, he said that he was ok with dying because I did not 'need' him and I would be ok. He said if he died tomorrow, he would be happy because he got to see me thriving on every level. I listened and I knew he was telling me because it was the truth AND he was so proud of me. He also did not know if he would ever be able to tell me again. Soon after, his speech and other physical functions declined rapidly.

I will end this two-part true love story by saying that David had a purpose and it was fulfilled. He wanted to make a massive impact and contribute something meaningful. He wanted his life to matter and he got what he wanted, and he gave so much more. He gave it to all of us. He touched our hearts and our lives. He changed us. He will continue to change many, many more and will have a lasting impact, as he desired. I will carry that out for him. You will carry that out for him. We will carry on his legacy and continue to pass it on. I love you, David, always and forever.

It made the most sense to have David's celebration of life event at our Cambridge home, "The House of Gathering". There were too many policies and restrictions on a place of business. Our home had a huge outdoor area in the back where tents and heaters were set up to accommodate all guests. Uncle Matt's restaurant did the catering with his amazing staff members providing service and cleanup. David got what he wanted: his best friends, coworkers, and family members all together in commemorating and celebrating his life and the deep impact he made on each of our lives. Many tears were shed, and more love was spread. Even though I had lost my beloved, I was surrounded by his pure love and the blessings he bestowed upon me.

Power-Thought: A Wave in The Sea of Life

- ☀ The vast Universe is likened to an endless sea. Then what are we? You and I are a part of it all, a wave in the sea of life.

- ☀ A single wave arrives from the sea. A single wave shifts and changes and at some point, goes back into the sea. Another one comes and goes... Such is life.

- ☀ You are a single wave that emerged from the sea of life. You go through changes here on earth in your lifetime and at some point, you merge back into the sea.

- ☀ Knowing the two guarantees of coming and going, in the sea of life, it's best for you to ride your wave of life as best you can!

- ☀ Recognizing you are a single wave but not separate from the sea of life brings harmony to you and the world. Seeing yourself as a separate wave from the sea of life brings disharmony to you and the world.

- ☀ Look at the bigger picture and keep surfing your wave. Choose not to drown yourself in someone else's wave that has slipped back into the sea of life.

> *Power-Quote: "The Soul comes from without into the human body, as into a temporary abode, and it goes out of it anew...it passes into other habitations, for the Soul is immortal."*

~Ralph Waldo Emerson

The After Death Holidays

As the holiday season approached, I chose to keep celebrating David's thirty-year life wave. I attended every single holiday gathering on both sides of the family. Whatever his dad and mom were doing, I joined in. It was uplifting beyond belief. I even went as far as having more holiday festivities at my home, for friends! David's friends and family filled the massive void from his physical absence. They replenished David's presence and eased the heaviness of grief. David would be overjoyed to know he brought us all together and that was the greatest gift for the holidays.

David didn't leave me alone. He blessed me with his friends and family. So many beautiful reminders of him. Loss opened my arms to life. There was no room for judgment, only love. There are some who haven't accepted David's death and remain bitter and in pain. My door is always open with compassion and forgiveness. Although I lost my husband, lover, and best friend, I am not lost without him.

Power-Thought: Celebrate Life Every Day

- ☼ Fighting and resisting change, or what has happened in the past, impedes your ability to celebrate life every day, what is now, and what is to come.

- ☼ When we don't accept life and all it comes with, we are in a constant fight for something to be different. That is a painful existence. You will spend a lifetime hurting yourself and others.

- ☼ When you treat each day as a blessing, no matter the changes, challenges, losses, or gains, you recognize the gift and miracle of life.

- ☼ Being in celebration mode means you are in a perpetual state of appreciation and gratitude. Imagine how that would feel for you and those around you? Imagine what you would be contributing to the world!

- ☼ When you celebrate life every day, there is no room for hate, prejudice, blame, anger, resentment, fear, or unhappiness. Love remains.

> *Power-Quote: "Life is meant to be a celebration! It shouldn't be necessary to set aside special times to remind us of this fact. Wise is the person who finds a reason to make every day a special one."*

> **~Leo F. Buscaglia**

PHASE NINE

New Openings Plus New Beginnings

The Loft

Each new day, despite the losses, was cause for celebration. After the studio's doors were closed for good, I continued to teach and educate. I taught virtual yoga classes from inside of my home on the main floor. While many were not ready for in-person classes, for various reasons, others were. I invited a small number of my yoga family to film the class for the virtual viewing. I rearranged the entire living room. The fireplace that David's stepdad built and installed provided ambiance and warmth for a cozy yoga practice. Those who attended were grateful for the space and sense of community, as was I.

It was wintertime. Out of nowhere, Daniel asked if he could attend one of my classes. I was thrilled to have him. He joined us one Sunday morning. After class, he said, "why don't you film yoga in the loft?". That question stunned me. The loft space was where David and I had a vision for both of us and our future. Renovating the loft raised the value of the home, which David was always thinking about. We could film and record our courses and educate clients and students. We had a plan for the loft. When he died the loft plan died too.

David was at the height of his illness when the loft was being renovated. He asked me to take over making all the decisions from the carpet, ceiling fans, paint color, and light fixtures to the sink and toilet in the bathroom. If David had been well, designing the loft would have been a fun project for us. But he wasn't and I loathed every second of it. All the selections felt like huge unbearable tasks for me to complete. They were stressful. I was in no shape for interior design while holding on for dear life and taking care of my husband. The loft was right over the master bedroom. There was pounding, hammering, drilling, and work being done daily for months on end. I had an ongoing migraine. By the time the loft was finished, I closed the door. It was too painful of an experience to reopen until Daniel asked that question. I was ready to reopen that door and release my buried anger. Upon climbing up the narrow stairs as if entering an undiscovered territory, beautiful and charming space was discovered! My eyes welled up with tears of unexpected glee from reopening a door. The perfect private yoga loft workspace was born!

Power-Thought: Believe and Receive

- A believer is wide open to receiving. Without expecting anything, a believer receives everything and more.
- When you believe in yourself you are receptive. When you don't, you are closed to reception.
- By believing in yourself you see possibilities and opportunities and they see you!
- The power of self-belief alone opens doors to more.
  - Believing is Receiving.
  - If you are not receiving, you are not believing in yourself.
  - Disbelieving in yourself blocks your reception.

Power-Quote: "There's nothing you can't achieve as long as you believe".

~Caren Paskel

The Waiting Room

My self-belief was opening new doors. The loft had an enclosed adequate area for private yoga, filming virtual yoga, another smaller room I named, "the waiting room" plus a charming bathroom. A mini yoga sanctuary. The waiting room had a large window that lit up the room and revealed Mother Nature. This room turned into a very special place; my dedicated personal creative space. When I began working with my mentors, they asked me if I had my own space for my energy and creativity to flow freely. At the time, I did not. My home was gigantic. There was no excuse. One of my mentors said, "that room is awaiting YOU, Caren!" I stepped into my new room and played, like a child. Moving things around, hanging my artwork on the walls, and making it feel wonderful to be in.

Once my very special, playful, and creative environment was set up, I was immediately inspired to create! Only three months into a 12-month mentorship journey, I rolled out a 12-month *Mental Training Mentorship. Mental Training 2.0; The Play-Ground Paradigm* was birthed from self-belief. Daniel gave me a desk and helped me set up an extra computer screen of David's for live presentations. I started taking coaching calls and facilitating *Mental Training Community Support Calls* in the waiting room. The entire loft became a small Spiritual haven. The waiting room became a place for my personal growth, transformational coaching calls, *Mental Training* presentations, and the creation of more to come.

Power-Thought: Make A Shift That Lifts

- ☼ A paradigm is a standard, perspective, or framework. A set of ideas or a way of looking at something.

- ☼ For there to be a paradigm shift there has to be a shift at every single level. There must be a different thought, feeling, and action.

- ☼ For your best self and life, ensure that your paradigm shift lifts you up and those around you.

- ☼ Go down the list to make a shift that lifts:

    - ⊙ What's your environment like?

    - ⊙ What shape and health are your physical body in?

    - ⊙ What is your mind entertaining?

    - ⊙ What is your intellect entertaining?

Caren Paskel

> *Power-Quote: "A simple paradigm shift is all it takes to change the course of your life forever."*

-Jeff Spires

The Solo Getaways

Before building out *Mental Training 2.0*, I planned on traveling to India and spending time with my gurus for a longer stay. A three-month journey to *The Vedanta Academy* in Pune was my plan. Due to the pandemic, obtaining a visa and traveling to India wasn't a possibility. As an alternative, per my mentors' suggestion, I decided on solo getaways for Spiritual expansion. The time away from what was familiar and comfortable empowered my relationship with myself. Tuning into my abilities and learning to fully trust myself. Going away alone allowed for personal bonding to the one source of true happiness, my self-belief.

The first solo getaway was approximately a three-hour drive from my home. Onyx and I took off for five nights and six days. We stayed in a tiny Airbnb, in the middle of nowhere. I planned on doing nothing on purpose and it was marvelous! Being mentally relaxed does not mean being lazy or inactive. It means the mind is quieted, disturbance-free without needing or wanting anything in particular to do. It's about BEing rather than DOing! From this mental stance, each day unfolded effortlessly and beautifully. Onyx and I went on adventures, exploring trails behind the little house. We came across a huge piece of land that held beautiful horses. The horses perked up at the sight of Onyx and came running toward us from across the field. He sprinted back and forth as the horses joined in galloping. It was like a movie scene. What a surprise! We visited them daily. Feeling playful and believing in myself created the most incredible experiences. It was as though I was standing still and life came to me. I planned another solo getaway for the next month.

Onyx and I packed up the car for a solo getaway round two. This time I chose to go to a little town that David and I had traveled to for Nan and her David's small wedding. When they got married, they told us what they were doing and it sounded so fun we invited ourselves! They were elated to have us and we all had the best time. The memory was a lovely one. I thought about creating another fantastic experience on my own this time. Onyx and I walked into town every day attracting all kinds of people.

Onyx brings so much joy to people, children, and other dogs. We met all sorts of interesting beings. The town was dog friendly. We went out for dinner together on the water. Oh, what fun we had. Onyx was such a good boy! He was a wonderfully hilarious, sweet, affectionate, and very slobbery date. We had such pleasant dining out. We went to the dunes and broke the rules. In the offseason, the beach was empty. We ignored the huge sign that read "no dogs allowed". Onyx ran up and down the dunes and frolicked on the shoreline. We both were so happy.

The solo getaways made me stronger and more independently happy. I desired self-sufficiency, fully free and happy, no matter what or who would be coming or going. I had to push myself further. The next trip needed to be further away. It was time to take flight by myself and go somewhere luxurious. It was my time to shine and be a bright butterfly queen!

Power-Thought: The World Is a Playground

- ☀ Give yourself space to play. Your playfulness exists within you and that's where the magic happens.

- ☀ When you make space to play, the world becomes a giant playground for you to play on every day of your life. How fun! You may fall but you will laugh it off, dust yourself off and continue to play all day.

- ☀ Be curious about your life and how you can shape your future. Explore all of your options and possibilities, imagine and dream.

- ☀ Think about children at play. When and where did that go, and why? Children play all day and so can YOU.

- ☀ Live in the spirit of playfulness and act like an adult to avoid getting yourself into trouble.

- ☀ Figure out how to have the best time with yourself so that you don't need anyone else to do so. Vacation with another, others, OR even better YOURSELF.

The Power of Self-Belief

- ☀ Mental stress kills your ability to be playful.

- ☀ When you give the mind space to relax you attract incredible experiences that are unexpected and most enjoyable.

- ☀ With the power of self-belief, life is magical and playful.

> *Power-Quote: "We don't stop playing because we grow old; we grow old because we stop playing."*

~George Bernard Shaw

The Home Alone

The solo getaways brought a newfound playfulness home with me. Spending quality time with myself prepared me for the inevitable, living in my house alone again. It was only a matter of time before Daniel moved out. Caregiving replaced his college campus life experience. Instead, he took classes online. David's death was crushing. Residing for another year together was essential for our healing and grieving. We were compatible housemates and change would have been devastating for us both. Within the year after the loss, I was becoming much stronger in being alone without needing to constantly be surrounded by David's friends and family. Daniel's presence sufficed and was enough for me to be ok. There was a sense of safety in having him there after David's death. I could sleep at night and felt like David was still alive. He was the little brother I never had, and we became very close, especially going through such an intense situation of having to care for David together. We were a team. He was strong when I was weak and visa-versa.

Daniel and I went through similar yet very different processes with life after David's death. My career was gaining momentum. The power of my self-belief was reviving and recreating my business and personal relationships. My entire life was transforming. The way through grief was to focus on my life. Finding my way led Daniel in finding his way too. I never told him what to do unless he asked for my opinion. Being supportive of his ideas brought him energy and excitement. It wasn't

Caren Paskel

my business to tell him what to do or how to do it. I took care of myself every day and planted the seeds for my future ahead. He began to take care of himself. He started to gain more health and happiness and think about his future! It was time for him to move on and so he did. He moved out. The next phase of time had come to be apart and explore what was in store. We each had a life to be lived. The move-out allowed forward movement. Because of our tight bond and open communication, we worked through the emotional transition. At first, Daniels's absence felt like David had disappeared. My home felt empty and there was a void. Holding on was not healthy for either of us. I had to believe in myself to live happily alone. Initially, it took some time to get used to. With growth, there's outgrowth and we had outgrown living together but that didn't mean it was easy to go our separate ways. Being alone is powerful in itself.

Power-Thought: Lead the Way

- The most effective and powerful way to make any kind of change in others is to lead the way by your example.

- When you try to tell or force others to change that will backfire. Trying to get someone else to do what you believe is correct is ineffective. If you know it's not working, why are you doing it?

- MYOB! By minding your own business, you will be able to set the right example without being upset or bothered by what others are doing or not doing.

- If you truly want to help someone, first and foremost, they have to be willing to be helped! Ask these three questions before you try and help:

  - Are they willing to be helped?

  - Are they wanting your help?

  - Have they asked for your help?

- If you tell someone what to do, that you are not doing, everything you say loses all power. You are a hypocrite!

- Ask yourself, are you modeling what you are teaching or preaching? If not, shut up and figure out how to live it.
- If you want to educate or teach, it's not about pushing or shoving your ideas on or in. The word educate means to draw out. Most educational systems do the very opposite. Most parents and leaders do the same. You will be frustrated in your pursuit and your actions will be futile!
- When you lead the way, you automatically influence and guide those around you.

> *Power-Quote: "What you do has far greater impact than what you say."*

-Stephen Covey

PHASE TEN

Full Unveiling Plus Double Metamorphosis

The Vail Trip Together

My parents exposed me to family travel experiences and activities throughout my childhood. I was fortunate to learn how to ski at the age of five. Our ski trips started in Northern Michigan and escalated to Snowmass, Steamboat, Aspen, and Vail Colorado. I have vivid and wonderful memories of our family ski vacations. The smell of the clean mountain air, snow falling on my face, riding up the gondolas, cruising down the slopes, lunching midday on the mountain, warming up by the fireplace at the end of the day, and soaking in the whirlpool under the stars at night. It was heavenly. Vail was exquisite from the splendid town with luxury shopping, wonderful food, and places to eat at the gorgeous hotels and the most magnificent mountain for skiing. I wanted to taste and share this remarkable experience with David. In December of 2016, we booked our first extravagant ski trip to Vail, Colorado!

Our hotel, *The Sebastian*, was spectacular with an art gallery, multiple restaurants, shops, a gym, and a spa. David had minimal ski skills. I insisted we take a ski lesson and he declined as he enjoyed the thrill of learning from living. Extreme weather conditions made skiing more challenging on the first morning. But we still had a blast! We had lunch on the mountain to fuel and warm up. David might have told this next part of the story differently. We got ready to go skiing the second half of the day. David stopped on the slope to adjust something, his hat or goggles. Whatever it was, he was parked on the mountain, standing still, and then toppled over. The way he fell twisted his ankle. He rejected

Caren Paskel

my idea for a ski patrol and painfully skied down the mountain. That was it for skiing!

David's swollen ankle did not deter us from having the time of our lives without skiing! We shopped, wined, and dined at the top restaurants in town, had a spa day, went snowshoeing and the most radical was snowmobiling high up and deep into the mountains. Snowmobiling was a full day's excursion. The beauty combined with the buzz of racing through the fresh powder and immense trees in the wilderness was breathtaking and incredibly fantastic! Our giant snowsuits helped barrier the freezing temperatures. On the return, I became quite cold. The guide recommended driving to warm back up. To start, I was timid but not for long! Feeling more alive than ever, we were ripping through the mountains and giggling with David behind me, holding me tight.

David's ankle improved over the next couple of days. I thought that snowboarding might be better for his footing and easier for him than skiing. We decided on trying it and taking a lesson together. Snowboarding came naturally for David. He was having a great time while I was falling on my ass repeatedly. If his life wasn't cut short, he would have for sure become a badass snowboarder. Whatever David set his mind on, he would accomplish or achieve. He lived a dream life because he believed in himself to do so. He took me with him for the ride. When he died, I kept on dreaming while I was awake for both of us.

The Power of Self-Belief

Power-Thought: Dream While You're Awake

- ☀ Dreams, while you are sleeping, are your unconscious and undigested thoughts. Although your mind is active in your dreams, you are unable to control your thoughts.

- ☀ Dreams, while you are awake, are your conscious thoughts that produce your actions.

- ☀ Thoughts precede actions and actions proceed with thoughts. This is why it's so very important to think about what you are thinking about!

- ☀ Your thoughts are planting your action seeds. Continue to water and nurture your thought seeds for them to grow and flourish into your dream life.

- ☀ Dream or envision the life you want to live while you are awake!

> *Power-Quote: "The life of your dreams, everything you would love to be, do or have, has always been closer to you than you knew, because the power to everything you want is inside you.*

~Rhonda Byrne

The Vail Trip Alone

David taught me to make life happen from me rather than to me or for me. Five years later, after our Vail trip together, I booked my Vail trip alone in February 2022. Unlike my solo getaway with Onyx, I was ready to fully embody the brilliant butterfly being I had become. This was the first time I had ever made big travel plans by myself. Self-belief gave me the confidence to book the flights, shuttles, stay, lift tickets, ski rentals, and find my way around. I made dinner reservations and navigated the town solo. It was truly exhilarating! I did it all on my own.

With the power of self-belief, I fully showed up and unveiled my authentic self. Stepping outside at Eagle airport, soaking in the sun that shined brightly in the giant bluest sky, felt invigorating. A friendly shuttle driver asked where I was staying. When I mentioned *The Tivoli*

Lodge, he commented, "wow, if you are staying there, you must be some kind of millionaire or something?" I laughed and replied with a smile, "not quite but I'm on my way". On the way to the hotel, I sat up front and made friends with the driver. I used to go out of my way to hide and avoid conversations at all costs, especially with strangers. Who was this new person? The power of self-belief made instant connections.

My hotel room wasn't ready upon arrival. By three o'clock I was starving. Leaving my bags behind, I strolled into town. There it was, *Sweet Basil,* the first place David and I ate for dinner on our Vail trip together. Unfortunately, they would not be serving dinner until five o'clock.. Since the bar was open, I sat down to enjoy a glass of wine and made friends with the bartenders. The bar was empty. Having their full attention, I shared my story about my late husband and how we had found this very spot together. As I went to pay for my drink, the nice man said, "this one's on us, we are touched by your story and sharing your memory with us." Tears filled my eyes. They allowed me to save my seat at the bar to come back for dinner!

Caren Paskel

Power-Thought: Share Your Story

- 🔆 When you are an open book, others will want to read! They will be intrigued and want to know what you are all about. Not only that, they will open up to share their story as well.

- 🔆 Everyone has a story but most keep it to themselves. Nobody wants to be around a closed book!

- 🔆 You don't need to go shout out and tell your story to everyone. Sharing your story is an attitude you carry with you. It's an openness you give off that attracts others to you.

- 🔆 Conversations begin and deep connections are made by sharing your story.

- 🔆 The more connections you make, the more alive you feel. The more alive you feel will awaken many more around you.

> *Power-Quote: Your story is the key that can unlock someone else's prison. Share your testimony."*

> **~Spiritual Inspiration**

The Brain Cancer Connections

Believing in myself made sharing and connecting with perfect strangers easy-breezy. After a full day of travel, without a shower or change of clothes, shopping was in order. There was a shop conveniently next door to the restaurant. I walked out of the store in a new outfit! Refreshed, hungry, and perfect timing for dinner! The place was packed and the bar seating was full. My saved seat was awaiting. I wedged myself in next to a friendly-looking couple. Within minutes we started chatting. Upon sharing coming to Vail alone, they listened as children do when they are being read a good story. Coincidentally, the man's name was David. When mentioning that my husband had died at a young age of brain cancer, he asked "was it glioblastoma?" He was an infectious disease doctor and his wife Denise, sitting next to him, worked in neurology. They were aware of the terminal brain cancer that

The Power of Self-Belief

David had. What they exposed next blew my mind. David the Doctor looked at his wife and said, "Denise, why don't you tell her what happened to you." Denise opened up about her story to me. She was a brain cancer survivor. Just like my David, she underwent surgery that left a giant moon-shaped scar across her entire head and had experienced compromised health with seizures, treatments, and medications… This first dining experience alone was filled with incredible shared stories, love, tears of gratitude, empathy, and new friendships. We exchanged numbers and embraced before returning to our hotels. Denise and I stayed in touch and met up for a drink a few nights later. It was as though we were friends for years. I made good friends on the very first day of my trip to Vail alone. Who was this social butterfly? It was me, emerging from a cocoon, and flying freely.

The very next evening, entering a beautiful ski shop, I was greeted by a gleeful lady named Winter. My eyes were lured to bright red ski pants. Winter helped me find the right size. I was an open book and so was she! We instantly connected and discovered that we had a lot in common. She had gone through a type of brain cancer that was in the frontal lobe of her brain. She went blind from this form of cancer for some time. Thankfully, she had surgery and recovered. Her spirit and energy radiated. We were teary-eyed exchanging brain cancer stories over the register. I left the store that night with way more than an amazing pair of ski pants. The beautiful bond with another being was priceless.

On my last day, my legs and ankles were screaming. I had ski-legs. I decided to call it quits at lunchtime. There was one highly recommended restaurant where reservations were impossible to make. It was called *Mountain Standard*. Being single, I strolled in and found a seat at the bar. The bartender and a few of the customers surrounding me were extremely friendly. We were all conversing and laughing while eating great food. Everyone, including the bartender, was treating me to drinks.

Caren Paskel

A wonderful lady and her daughter sat next to me while they waited for their table. They turned down the table and stayed at the bar with me. It was the daughter's birthday. She was thirty-seven and her mom was taking her out to celebrate. After talking with them, they were hooked on my story. The daughter then shared with me that she was diagnosed with multiple sclerosis She had two young children and a lovely husband. Her disease is under control, and she is doing well. She also shared a brain cancer story with me. They knew a local entrepreneur. Jeff Brausch lived in Vail with his wife and three children. He recently passed away from glioblastoma. Within hours we became familial. I left with a beaming and contagious smile. Spreading so much love and cheer all around with everyone was incredibly uplifting and gifting.

Power-Thought: Spread Cheer Over Fear

- Cheer and fear are both contagious. Which one do you want to spread?
- When you walk around in cheer, you spread more cheer! When you walk around in fear, you spread more fear.
- Cheer lifts you and others up while fear brings you and others down.
- Think about how you walk and talk. What attitude, energy, and vibration do you carry and give off?
  - ⊙ Are you infecting others with your cheer or fear?
- Emanating cheer attracts cheerful people.
- Fear holds you hostage and robs cheer and joy in your life.
- Stay clear of fear and spread your cheer!

> *Power-Quote: "What sunshine is to flowers, smiles are to humanity. These are but trifles, to be sure; but scattered along life's pathway, the good they do is inconceivable."*

~Joseph Addison

The Ski Tours

Cheerfulness and spontaneity led me from one amazing experience to another. When David and I were in Vail we went to a divine French cuisine restaurant called. I remembered the decor and food but not the name. The first night at *Sweet Basil*, I asked the bartender what the top restaurants were. He mentioned *La Tour* first. The name sounded familiar. I made a reservation for the next night and it was indeed the place David I savored! My table was next to the window. A very cute and delightful waiter went over the menu with me. Of course, we connected! After dining was complete, he offered to take me on a tour of the mountain the next day. He said he would be happy to do so. The next day we met up at gondola number one and had a magnificent day. He took a fabulous picture of me on top of the mountain with my red-hot ski pants. On the first run down, he took a spill. Turns out he was a beginner skier. It was a gorgeous day and the sun softened the snow. We skied all over the mountain and in-between the trees. On the chairlifts, we talked about life. He asked me questions about yoga which made the tour even more fun for me! We had a blast. Afterward, as a thank you, I offered him the amazing cookies at my hotel and a beer before parting ways. I felt like I gifted him some knowledge with my presence and in exchange, I learned how to navigate the mountain for the rest of my ski trip!

The next day, I was ready for more exploration. Upon riding up the gondola midday after lunch there were two nice men. We got to talking. One man seemed to know the mountain well. We ended up skiing together for the rest of the day! He extended an invitation to join him and his friend that evening at *The Slope Room* which happened to be right around the corner from where I was staying. This was the same night I met Denise at my hotel for happy hour. Thereafter, I went to meet more new friends and found the perfect seat for myself at the bar. My new friends showed up. Simultaneously two spots on each side of me opened up. We proceeded to have a wonderful time chatting, eating good food, drinking fine wine, and sharing our stories! After our meal,

Caren Paskel

it was bedtime for me. When I went to pay my bill, my new friends unexpectedly treated me. What a gift!

Power-Thought: You Attract What You Are

- ☀ Notice who you have attracted over the course of your life. What kind of shape were you in physically, mentally, intellectually, and spiritually?

- ☀ The power of self-belief is magnetizing. You will attract those who wish to be around and are inspired by your energy. They are good and want to be influenced in a positive way.

- ☀ When you are falling apart, stressed out, miserable, or unhappy, be cautious. You attract what you are. The combination is most likely destructive and detrimental.

- ☀ It's best to pick yourself up and do the work to make improvements on yourself.

- ☀ When you start believing in your best self, you will become your best self.

- ☀ Self-belief draws a different type of person, one that is worthy of your presence and will treat you that way.

- ☀ The power of self-belief magnetizes the most beautiful souls.

> *Power-Quote: "What you radiate outward in your thoughts, feelings, mental pictures and words, you attract into your life."*
>
> **~Catherine Ponder**

The Butterfly Queen

The brilliant, beautiful butterfly flies around, with its artistic wings delightfully enchanting anyone who may be around. Landing here and there, revealing its bright beauty and unique essence. The mysteriously stunning creature, having gone through a metamorphosis, is gloriously free. The power of self-belief blossomed me into a Butterfly Queen that flutters and frolics. Without anticipation or particular plans, my entire escapade was blissful. As a butterfly presence, I sprinkled love and light. My self-belief was exposed as a polished gem. The power radiated like a lighthouse. Being present was a gift to myself and those I met along the way. Magnificent beings were drawn toward my light on my Vail trip alone. There was no more dependence on my husband's power of self-belief. The power of self-belief shined through. His and mine were integrated, a double metamorphosis.

Caren Paskel

Power Thought: Your Light Brightens the World

- ☀ When you are a bright light your beautiful glistening light beams onto the world around you. Be the light that brightens.

- ☀ The source of all beings is light. Where darkness prevails, there is uncovered light. Your job in life is to uncover and discover your inner light source. As you do you bring light and love to the world.

- ☀ When your light is dimmed or seemingly turned off, the entire world will seem dark.

- ☀ Your light leadership inspires and enlightens.

Power-Quote: "Be the light you want to brighten the world with."

-Caren Paskel

PHASE ELEVEN

The Power of Self-Love to Be Continued...

The Love After Loss

The coalescence of self-belief and self-love is revolutionary. You will be living in an overflow of abundance that greatly impacts the world. The power of self-belief enables your greatest potential within. The power of self-love enables your purest love within. Your lifelong soulmate, that remains, is YOU! Soulmates are an effect of believing and loving yourself. You will never be alone even when someone you love passes away. Their energy, love, and light will be with you in other ways than physical presence.

One searches for and seeks external love when they are lacking internal love. The power of self-belief and self-love filled me up and did not perish with my husband. I wasn't looking for another relationship nor was there a desire to pursue anyone or be pursued. My new mental shift lifted me and kept me moving forward. While valuing companionship and partnership in many ways, I wasn't in need or wanting that to be happy or successful. This was an empowering position and stance to be in. I wanted everything I already had!

The power of my thriving self-belief and love drew even more love into my life that I never saw coming. It was there all along as if the love was simply not lost. The power of self-belief and self-love manifested in a more intimate yoga community and deeply committed clients. Friendships evolved. A new relationship was born from a shared loss. An unexpected life experience brought two very unpredictable and odd souls together in an extremely helpful and healing way. Many may not understand how I could have and feel so much love after losing the love of my life. Self-belief and love persist, that's how. My love was alive and grew stronger. If I stopped loving that would stop me from living. There is love in my life because I love myself. David's love for me was infinite. He wanted me to keep living, loving, and to be happy after he was gone. That's the truth he told me.

There are no worries about what lies ahead. Self-belief and self-love defeat and conquer all loss. My self-love is all I truly need and anything on top of that is extra. When David was first diagnosed with brain cancer I reached out to my guru. She replied:

Challenges come to make you strong and not weaken you. You have come into this world by yourself. That's the way you will go. In between meeting and living with people and circumstances. Good and bad. Right and wrong. Watch them come into your life, stay awhile and perhaps change or even leave. You need to go on your journey of life by yourself. But let me assure you... you are not alone! You go on till you find the Truth.

I hold these words dear and true to me and so may any being who wishes to live an exceptional and extraordinary life.

Power-Thought: You Hold the Key to Unlock Your Heaven

- ☼ The power of self-belief leads you to the ultimate Truth and Love within yourself.

- ☼ You and your life will evolve in ways you never dreamed or imagined possible.

- ☼ Everything you could ever dream of or want is already inside of you and you have the keys to unlock your heaven. Your heaven awaits.

- ☼ Believe in yourself and you will live and let live, love and let love, and be free to be the brilliant butterfly that you are.

Power-Quote: "The possibilities of your life and in the world are endless and inevitable through the power of self-belief and self-love."

-Caren Paskel

About the Author

Caren Paskel's life's purpose and fulfillment are to Spiritually Educate through Master Storytelling. She is the Founder of *Mental Training*. Using yoga principles and philosophy, she evokes others to transform into fearless, independent, and radiant leaders. Caren has achieved abundant happiness and believes that it is every human's birthright.

After many years working within the yoga community and with limited business experience, Caren became sole proprietor of the popular and successful *EnSoul Yoga* studios in Ferndale and Detroit. While preparing to open a third studio, a seismic shift occurred: her husband became terminally ill and there was a global pandemic. This required a total pivot in her business and personal life.

Where there was a difficulty, Caren created opportunity. Through workshops, training, storytelling, and one-on-one interactions, Caren shares her inspirational story of overcoming extreme adversity to metamorphose into a confident, capable human, and light leader.

Engaging in *Mental Training* mentorship and courses, paired with her personal experiences navigating and rising above challenges and losses, encouraging and inspiring clients to change from within, take action, and become impactful. Caren continues to manifest her true calling and is living her dream life. She is making positive change and leadership within the community to create a universal ripple effect.

Caren continues to work on her self-development to transform herself, others, and the world in a practical, playful, and tough-loving way.

Resources

- 💡 *https://www.vedantaworld.org/*
- 💡 *https://carenpaskel.com/mentaltrainingcourse*
- 💡 *https://www.facebook.com/groups/spiritualeducationforum*
- 💡 *Can't Doesn't Exist* by David Prentice and Joshua Gordon

Love this book? Don't forget to leave a review!

Every review matters, and it matters a *lot!*
Head over to Amazon or wherever you purchased this book to leave an honest review for me.
I thank you endlessly.

Made in the USA
Columbia, SC
02 March 2024

32563571R00089